ROBERT JAMES CERFOLIO, MD, MBA

SUPER
PERFORMING

AT W✚RK AND AT H⌂ME

The Athleticism
of Surgery and Life

RIVER GROVE
BOOKS

Published by River Grove Books
Austin, TX
www.rivergrovebooks.com

Distributed by River Grove Books

For ordering information or special discounts for bulk purchases, please contact
River Grove Books at PO Box 91869, Austin, TX 78709, 512.891.6100.

Design and composition by Greenleaf Book Group
Cover design by Greenleaf Book Group
Image Credits: Baseball Players: ©iStockphoto.com/ROBOTOK;
Man with Baseball and Glove: ©iStockphoto.com/EHStock;
Doctor: ©veer.com/stefanolunardi;

Publisher's Cataloging-In-Publication Data

Cerfolio, Robert.
   Super performing at work and at home: the athleticism of surgery and life/Dr.
Robert Cerfolio.—First edition.
    pages : illustration ; cm
   Issued also as an ebook.
   ISBN: 978-1-938416-80-4
   1. Cerfolio, Robert. 2. Surgeons—United States. 3. Success—Psychological
aspects. 4. Performance—Psychological aspects. 5. Sports—Psychological
aspects. 6. Time pressure. I. Title.
BF637.S8 C47 2014
158.1   2014938771

Printed in the United States of America on acid-free paper

14 15 16 17   10 9 8 7 6 5 4 3 2 1

First Edition

To my wife, Lorraine, and my three boys, Robby, Alec and Matthew—they are why I strive to super perform.

CONTENTS

INTRODUCTION—1

Why Am I Operating?

—∿∿∿—

Life: Take Nothing for Granted
Athleticism: Failing at
Crunch Time

CHAPTER ONE—7

Understanding Your Lines of Gratification

—∿∿∿—

Life: Building Blocks of Success
Athleticism: Developing the
Fundamentals of the Game

The Lines of Gratification—7

Be an Early Riser—12

For the Love of the Game—15

Did You Really Try Your Best?—17

Rub Some Dirt on It—21

Striving to Hit .400 Every Year—27

Setting Specific, Measurable Goals—30

Find the High Ground—31

Be the Go-To Guy—35

CHAPTER TWO—39

Enjoy the Long Bus Rides

......⌇⌇⌇⌇......

Life: Riding the Escalator of Life
Athleticism: Performing when the Spotlight Is Brightest

Fueling the Internal Flame of a Super Performer—39

Iverson Got It All Wrong—43

Forming Good Practice Habits—46

Hubris Hurts—48

Ignite the Internal and Eternal Flame—51

Always Choose the Highest Peak—54

It Ain't Over Until the Fat Lady Sings—58

Shining when the Lights Are Bright—64

CHAPTER THREE—69

Lifetime Commitment to Super Performing

......⌇⌇⌇⌇......

Life: Living in the Moment
Athleticism: Sweeping the Dirt Off the Rubber

Super Performing by Staying in the Moment—69

The "No Lose" Scenario—74

Super Performers Never Take a Vacation from Super Performing—79

A Major Injury Is Only One Play Away—81

The Fragility of Life—85

With One Swing of the Bat—88

Learn a New Pitch Every Season—95

The Rewards of Teaching—99

CHAPTER FOUR—103

Proper Preparedness

*Life: Responding to Adversity
with Mental Agility*

*Athleticism: Practicing the
Way We Play*

Prepare for Disaster—103

Practice the Way You'll Play—108

Efficient Practicing
via Videotaping—109

Rehabilitation Starts the Day
of Your Injury—113

Your Response to Adversity Is
What Defines You—117

CHAPTER FIVE—121

Getting and Staying
in the Zone

*Life: Thinking Like a
Super Performer*

*Athleticism: Blocking out
the Crowd Noise*

The Zone—121

Trust Your Pregame Routine—124

The Mind-set of a Super
Performer—126

Blocking Out the Crowd Noise—129

Adapting to Field Conditions—133

Strategies for Relaxation—134

Visualization—138

Keep It Simple—140

CHAPTER SIX—145

The Game Must Go On, and with Humility

------\/\/-------

Life: The World Keeps Spinning

Athleticism: Winning Without Your "A" Game

Know when to Bench Yourself—145

Super Performing when You Don't Have Your "A" Game—149

Keep Shooting—152

Pinnacle Performance—154

CHAPTER SEVEN—161

Pressure Equals Opportunity

------\/\/-------

Life: Keeping Family Connections

Athleticism: Shrinking the Lines of the Playing Field

Home Field Advantage—161

Staying Connected to Your Family—164

Check Your Ego at the Door—167

Why Do We Fall?—170

Why Don't Professionals Have Coaches?—172

They Can't Stop the Clock—176

Knowing when to Stop—178

Losing Is an Opportunity to Get Stronger—186

CHAPTER EIGHT—195

Super Performing Is Just
a Piece of the Puzzle

*Life: Super Performing to
Serve Others*

Athleticism: Losing with Grace

The Reason to Want to Be a
Super Performer—195

Understand Your Higher
Purpose—197

The Power of Prayer—205

Grace, Dignity, Humility, and
Faithfulness—208

Life and Death—212

EPILOGUE—225

The Mastery of
Pursuits That Offer
Endless Significance

ABOUT THE AUTHOR—229

INTRODUCTION

Why Am I Operating?

Take Nothing for Granted

. . .

Failing at Crunch Time

It was a Wednesday in June 2010. It was a typical day for me in the operating room. I had several visitors watching me operate, and I had eight operations, two in each of the four operating rooms that I have run for the past ten years.

The only difference was that today my wife of twenty years, Lorraine Bernadette, was also in a surgical operating room just two floors above me. Unfortunately, she was on the other end of the scalpel. Just a few days earlier, she had been diagnosed with breast cancer, and she was to undergo a mastectomy with a biopsy of the lymph nodes in her armpit. One lymph node is called a sentinel node, and it is generally one of the first sites breast cancer attacks. By checking the sentinel node for signs of cancer, doctors can determine whether it's likely that the cancer has begun to spread to the rest of the body. It was unlikely that it had in Lorraine's case, since the tumor was still very small, but in a real sense her medical fate would be determined by that test.

I took Lorraine in to the hospital early. I sat with her in the preoperative holding area for an hour. We talked, worried, and laughed together. We held hands, and then I watched her as they wheeled her off to surgery.

Then I went to do my job. I certainly was not going to sit in the waiting room and do nothing.

Just before the operation, one of my visitors, hearing about what Lorraine was about to undergo just above us, approached me.

"You mean to tell me that your wife is having breast cancer surgery upstairs right now," he asked me, "and you are down here doing eight operations? Why? Why would you do that? Why are you operating today?"

But I, like most surgeons, had never even considered canceling my operations. I had always done my job. I had always honored my professional and personal commitments, as most surgeons do every day. After all, my patients had cancer as well. They had families who had been praying for them as well. They were stressed as well. They needed surgery as well, and this date had been booked weeks in advance for all eight of them. I had to honor those commitments, didn't I? Today was no different than any other. I had several short operations that day and a few long ones. I had one particularly dangerous operation on a lung cancer patient. In the operation, called a pulmonary-artery sleeve resection of the left upper lobe, we take out the upper part of the left lung, or the left upper lobe. Because this patient's lung cancer was large and central, it was very close to the pulmonary artery, the very thin-walled but critical main artery that comes out of the heart. Because of this, we'd have to cut that artery in half in order to remove the cancerous part of the lung and then sew the artery back together. This allows the patient to keep the left lower lobe and be able to breathe better after surgery.

We were at the most critical part of the operation—placing a large clamp on the left main pulmonary artery as it exits the right side of the heart—when Lorraine's breast cancer surgeon came into my operating room. Despite her mask, she could not hide her concerned look, and the usual twinkle in her eye was absent.

As usual, I was not even patient enough to let her tell me her news first.

"Don't tell me that Lorraine's sentinel lymph node was positive. There's no way." I said this calmly as I turned my attention back to my operative field and finished cutting the pulmonary artery with precision and steady accuracy.

"Yes, Cerf—it was. I am so sorry," she said. "The good news is that the operation went well, and Lorraine is doing just great. The other lymph nodes all looked okay."

I was glad that the operation had gone well. Still, despite that and my outer calm, I was devastated. I knew what this meant: Lorraine, my beautiful, perfect, blond-haired, blue-eyed wife, did not have a simple stage-one breast cancer. Rather, it was going to be stage two. She would need chemotherapy, and her survival rate had just dropped from 95 percent to 85 percent.

We would forever be a cancer couple. A couple just like the ones I saw in my clinic every week. They held hands and their breaths in fear and in anticipation as I walked into the room and sat down next to them to give them the news of the chest CT scan that they had earlier in the day. They all prayed that I would tell them the same thing: that it was "all clear." Now, just like them, Lorraine and I would worry together the night before, hold our breath, and pray. We would wait for the doctor to come into our examining room and tell us the results, just as I have to do every day for my lung cancer patients.

Maybe my visitor had been right. Just why was I operating?

I peered down into my operative field through my magnifying glasses and headlight. Suddenly the well-lit, shallow, and inviting operative field that I had established just a moment ago looked dark, deep, and very dangerous. The pulmonary arterial walls that had just a moment ago appeared so thick and easy to sew now, in a split second, appeared paper thin. My confidence, my surgical judgment, and my skill, all of which had been so plentiful just a moment ago, were gone. For the first time in my professional life I could not perform—I could not operate.

Now what do I do? I could call one of the surgeons that are always available as backup during our operations, but I was not sure I needed them—yet.

How I got through this operation—as I'll try to teach you as I tell you my story—was to focus on the techniques, lessons, and strategies I had been relying on for my entire life; techniques I had learned from playing sports. I call it the athleticism of life: the practice that elevates the mind and body from good to great and that makes a star performer into a super performer. These lessons, strategies, and techniques are what I aim to share with you in this book, as well as a way to execute them in your life.

But that's not all I want to share. More importantly, in the years that followed that moment in the operating room, I learned much greater and more profound lessons, lessons that have helped me and that I hope will help you to strive to super perform in life—for the sake of the moment when you may find yourself, as I was, in your own operating room, wondering how to keep going forward.

CHAPTER 1

Understanding
Your Lines of Gratification

Building Blocks of Success

· · ·

Developing the Fundamentals of the Game

Forging the Metal

I am nothing special. But do not be fooled: I am not modest either. Despite my lack of great size, I was always incredibly confident between the lines of any playing field I set out on. And what I've learned over the years is how to make the game of life itself into a playing field—and how to achieve on that playing field, no matter the situation.

The Lines of Gratification

I was born in New Jersey in 1962. My dad was a urologic surgeon with a farmer's mentality, and my mom was a nurse with a mother's mentality. She believed she could win over the world with her personality and a positive attitude, and actually, she has.

My parents, like many parents of that time, inculcated a set of values in me and my three siblings that centered on the principles of hard work and perseverance. Many of these lessons were taught in the backyard and on the athletic field when I was young. Most still apply today now that I am older, and my playing fields are hospitals, operating rooms, and the chests of patients whom it's my job to heal.

What are some of these lessons? When I was eight years old, I was asked to join my dad and my older brother in the joy of cutting the backyard grass. All three of us would start off on Saturday morning, and my dad would assign each of us a section of the lawn to cut. It would take us about four hours in total to finish if we all worked together without stopping. We saved the clippings, which we spread over our garden to prevent weeds.

It became clear to me at eight that every time I went out with my dad and brother to cut the grass, I was going to be doing it for a while. So I decided to enjoy it. Specifically, I focused on the lines I made in the grass as the mower moved over it—the long parallel tracks made in the surface. These lines in the freshly mowed lawn—or the "lines of gratifica-tion," as I have come to call them over the years—were the end result of my hard work and sweat. The lines were mine. I did that; I had made them. My brother, dad, and I had done it together as a team. And thus, after a while, it was no longer just a task or an albatross. Rather, it was fun to make the lawn look good. This custodial task delivered satisfaction and pride.

Having learned the lesson when it came to mowing the lawn, I started to do the same thing with school and tests. A good grade at the top of a tough exam paper became as satisfying to look at as the lines that I had made in the lawn. Both gave me immediate feedback about the results of my hard work.

The simple boyhood task of cutting the lawn taught me a lot about life and work. I found that if I got up early and got the work done early, even if there was a slight dew on the lawn, somehow it seemed to take less time than when I did it later in the day. And somehow the day seemed longer, with more free time in it for me to play, than if I started later. The longer I procrastinated, the heavier the albatross got around my neck, and the longer the task seemed ultimately to take.

This truth about procrastination remained with me as I grew older and became a young physician. When I was a young surgical resident just out of medical school, we took call every other weekend, which meant that we would come in to make our rounds of the patients that we had operated on. Most residents wanted to take Saturday and Sunday to sleep late—which, for a surgical resident, means six a.m., because on weekdays rounds begin at four a.m. We had to see every patient, write orders and notes, and get to the operating rooms by seven. And the same rule was true then, some twenty years later, that I had learned in my backyard cutting the lawn as a boy. If we started early and worked as a team, somehow the day seemed longer and I had more free time than I would have if I had started later in the day—even when "later" meant six a.m. instead of four. Again, the work became fun.

Unlike most busy surgeons who are full professors at academic hospitals, I still stay after almost every surgery I perform to finish sewing the skin closed by using plastic surgical techniques. My incision marks in the skin are my new wheel marks in the lawn—my new lines of gratification. I still love the work, even after fifteen thousand operations. I still enjoy looking back and reveling in a beautiful subcuticular closure in the skin after we finish sewing the incision just right. I love to carefully scrutinize it. I almost never use staples or stitches that have to come out later, just as I would never shoot grass clippings on the lawn. After all, the incision is all the patient sees, just like the lawn is the first thing people see when they come to your house. It is how they judge your work.

There are many kinds of lines of gratification. For some, they are the number of zeroes in their bank statement; for others, they are the curves of their muscles after they leave the gym. It is good and healthy to look back to admire what you have accomplished and to revel in the fruits of your labor before moving on to the next task.

The key is to only do this briefly. Many people admire their own work too often and for too long. The reason to do it is not to gloat, but rather to help refuel yourself so that you can do more high-quality work the next day.

You should review your lines of gratification—your results—at set intervals. Each Christmas holiday, my team looks back at our operative log and reviews our results. I take pride in what I and my team have done well. But I also lament our—my—failures. Our failures in surgery are not losses on a playing field or on a financial spreadsheet; they represent the deaths of our patients. Each failure marks a death—or at least a major complication—for somebody's mom or dad, brother or sister, son or daughter. Some may not be avoidable—that is true—but we must always ask ourselves what we could have done differently. We strive to improve the process in order to improve the end result.

Failure, for you, might not mean death, but any company or business is no different. At the end of the fiscal year, review your final sheet, your cash flow, and your balance sheet. Each division should do the same. And the review should involve the results not just of your work life, but also of your family life. Parents should keep their children's old report cards and review them at set intervals in order to celebrate good grades (and to help determine what can be done to avoid bad ones in the future).

Be an Early Riser

Many of our surgical visitors from other countries—
especially our European visitors—are amazed at how early
our team starts operating in the morning. Our patients arrive
at the hospital around 5:30 a.m. and are in the operating
room by 7:00 a.m. We usually make our first incision in the
first operating room by 7:10 a.m. This is more than an hour
earlier than many of our visitors start. If you start early, you
finish sooner—just as I learned as a boy cutting the grass.
This leaves more time to do other work, go home earlier, and
eat dinner as a family.

But the major reason operating rooms start operating at
seven a.m. sharp is fundamentally tied to human physiology.
The human body is primed for stress and performance early
in the morning. In other words, the body of a patient is better
able to handle the stress of surgery at this time.

Since the surgeon, nurses, and other members of the
operating-room team are human as well, we are no different.
We perform best in the morning, so it's important—and our
society considers it important—to start work as early in the
morning as you can.

I get asked all the time: "Do you ever sleep?" I love to
sleep, just like everyone else. And despite my having learned
that mowing the lawn was easier the earlier in the day I
started, I never would have described myself when I was
young as a morning person. But after a few years of medical
school and surgical residency—a few years of waking up at

four a.m. most days, in other words—I became one. As I've gotten older, I can more readily detect my improved functionality earlier in the morning as well.

And, as I've grown older, I've come to accept more responsibility as a leader—which means I have to wake up earlier. The best way to foster the habit of being on time in your teammates is to lead by example. A leader has to be early and has to be one of the first ones to work, to a meeting, or to the operating room. That way, you can speak with authority when employees tell you that they're "not morning people." When employees tell me this, I tell them: "That's great; I am not, either. But our current society—and especially this hospital—mandates early-morning performance in most events. So you'd better learn how to function in the morning."

I tell them this because one of the most important concrete aspects of success is being on time. Some people fail at their jobs or other events in their lives simply because they are just not organized or disciplined enough to be on time. This single, simple logistical step may be one of the most important strategies for being successful. A golfer who climbs out of his car, rushes to the first tee, and pulls out his driver on the first hole will too often end up looking for his ball in the woods. A surgeon who is not physically or mentally prepared for an operation and who rushes to his first operating room will end up just as lost as that golfer—only the surgeon risks losing more than a golf ball.

So if you, like me once upon a time, don't currently

consider yourself a morning person, start becoming one. Immediately start developing the habit of being on time. If you find it hard to get out of bed in the morning, place your alarm clock far enough away from your bed so that you have to get out of bed to turn it off. Avoid hitting the snooze button more than once.

A child or teenager who continually oversleeps is a more difficult problem. Teenagers require more sleep than older adults; this is a physiologic fact. But letting them sleep until half the day is over (i.e., ten or eleven a.m.) is not the solution. You can start to break the cycle of sleeping late on weekends by getting your kids up early on Sunday morning so that they are more likely to be tired by ten p.m. on Sunday night. Our neighbors laughed at me, but Lorraine and I always had our kids get up earlier and earlier toward the end of our vacation. By getting our three boys up just a little bit earlier each day, they grew tired at nighttime, and they were ready to start school. Once they were seven or eight, we began to make them get themselves up out of bed, and we resisted the urge, as parents, to get them up. If they overslept, we let them suffer the consequence, and they quickly learned the habit we wanted them to learn.

In a corporation, you can't choose when your employees go to bed. But you can give each employee a report card for being on time and then have a monthly meeting where everyone's results are shown publicly on a slide, displayed from the best to the worst for all to see. This will add some competition to the mix and make people publicly responsible. There is no better way to change behavior or culture then public accountability and the public reporting of results of performance. A public track record for being at work on time can become a new line of gratification for the people who work for you.

For the Love of the Game

When I was a young boy, my family would often take a three-to four-day vacation at the Jersey shore. I enjoyed one particular hotel because the hotel's child-care program would give out multiple awards. The awards—tiny plastic trophies—were given out for various competitions among the kids in the program, most of them physical challenges. And every time we stayed at the hotel, I was determined to get as many of them as I could.

I recall practicing my flip on the hotel's diving board the day before the big event. Each time I got to the end of the board, I would yell to my mom and dad, who were sitting at the side of the pool, reading and trying their best to pretend I was not with them. Still, I begged them, I implored them to watch me jump and dive. "Mommy, Daddy look at me, watch me!" I screamed across the crowded pool deck. I was excited to have the opportunity to perform in front of a crowd, especially one with my parents in it.

And the next day, the hard work paid off. I won awards for building the best sand castle, doing the best flip off the diving boards, and achieving first place in the swimming races. In the races, I was competing against, at most, two other kids my age, both of whom could barely swim a stroke, and as my dad tells it now, I was the only kid in the front-flip event.

The tiny plastic trophies I won probably cost the hotel about fifty cents each. They were so cheap that one of the handles on the cup broke off even before I got it back to our hotel room. Despite their small stature and low cost, to me these trophies were priceless. I lined them up in my bedroom, and they created one of my earliest lines of gratification in my life.

Trophies and awards, as we've discussed, are a vital line of gratification, and the effort to win them is the best way to create a culture of hard work and enthusiasm in your team. But that culture can only be created if you can see the awards you've won. My oldest son, Robby, was recruited by several Division One baseball teams. During his official visits to the schools, I was amazed at how many schools had their championship trophies hidden in elaborate trophy cases or ornate rooms that few students had routine access to or could even see. The trophies should be displayed in locations where student athletes can see them each day on their way to the field or to the gym. Ensure that the ones who are doing the daily hard work that is required to win another championship get to see the fruits of that hard work every day.

Recently I accepted an award on behalf of my outstanding thoracic surgical team at the University of Alabama at Birmingham (UAB) for having the lowest observed-to-expected mortality ratio of all the medical and surgical services at our world-renowned institution. This is a great accomplishment for our team, given the sick and elderly patients we operate on every day and the complex operations we perform. We accomplished this honor through teamwork, and a key component of that is exuberance—the same exuberance I felt when I was competing for front-flip trophies as a child. Most visiting surgeons who come to watch us are amazed at the exuberance our team has as we go from one operating room to another. Most surgeons get only one operating room a day, and most operate three times a week, which means they perform two to three operations a day and six to nine per week. For many years I have had three to four operating rooms a day and operate four days a week. In each room we strive as a team to deliver the best performance we can for the patient.

Did You Really Try Your Best?

Perhaps the most overused and inaccurate phrase is "I tried my best." I hear this way too often. Are you sure? Are you really sure you could not have worked a little bit harder one day at practice or studied for just ten more minutes one day?

Success comes to those, a team or unit, who all share a goal and a similar set of values. The entire concept of succeeding or winning at something comes down to the definition of success, or what the goal is. It depends on how clearly success is defined by the team members, how accurately it is measured, and how badly the athlete or performer wants it.

Our team has achieved the awards it has because we're willing to look at our behavior and do what it takes to optimize it—not just to settle for "trying our best." For example, another thing that sometimes surprises our visitors: We work all day long without long breaks. Because we've created a culture of enthusiasm, we've defined "success" to mean a certain level of performance—a certain number of operations per day with the lowest rate of mortality possible. We know that in order to achieve that level, we need to work as hard and as efficiently as we can until the work is done. Breaks often serve only to add inefficiency and interrupt the work flow. So, because we want that level of success badly enough, we get by with a few five-minute breaks at ten a.m. and two p.m. that consist only of a protein shake, a P90X protein bar, and a glass of water—which is all you really need to keep going until the work is done if you've had a large, healthy breakfast.

The culture around you determines how you and your team define success and how you define "trying your best." The culture can be a family (parents usually set the tone of the culture), a team (the coach and owner set the tone), or a business (the board of directors sets the tone). The idea of achieving well-defined goals must be so ingrained in the athlete, performer, child, or employee that it becomes part of who they are. In other words, excellence and super performing must become fundamental to who they are and what they want to be. It must become part of their DNA, an intertwined fiber in their own musculo-skeletal system.

So what do you do if people on your team—athletes, performers, children, employees—don't share your values of super performing?

It is easier to create a value system early in a person's life than later, but the latter is still possible. One key is to try to recapture the feeling of exuberance found in childhood—the "Look at me, Mommy and Daddy" attitude. When I was practicing flips off the diving board at our hotel, I had no fear of failing. I was too busy thinking about the joy of performing in front of my loved ones. No matter how I performed—no matter how bad my flip off the diving board was that day—they loved me. It's the same with learning any skill, right down to learning to walk: No one belittled you if you lost your balance and fell down. The surrounding environment was one of unconditional love and nurturing. The outcome didn't matter as much as the effort and the process toward the outcome.

The key to cultivating a culture of enthusiasm—or to reforming those who don't fit easily into that culture—is to create that same type of environment. This holds true whether you're talking about a surgical team or about a child's big game or big test.

But obviously, a nine-month-old child who falls down while learning how to walk is quite different from an employee or teammate who makes a big mistake at a critical moment. Your goal as a leader and super performer is to ensure that this person recognizes his or her mistake, admits it, and is willing to change the process to get a better outcome next time.

A major part of doing that is to find the right words of affirmation that will lead them to desire to make the correction that leads to a better outcome—that creates the culture of enthusiasm that lies at the foundation of super performance. Your job is to create a team atmosphere that fosters this type of process and not one that condemns and blames teammates publicly or in the confines of the organization. Therefore, when a mistake is made and it is discussed at your group meeting, never discuss the individual's mistake—rather, discuss the process itself. Do not assign individual blame so much as identify the problem with the process or the system. If necessary, you should also talk to the individual in private about their personal mistake. If they have a record of working toward the team's desired level of excellence, they should be given another chance. (However, if mistakes continue, then they do need to be told that they do not fit into your organization because they do not share your value set— unless, of course, the team is your family and the individual is a family member!)

One way to help motivate your team members is to show them the specific rewards of what you and your team have accomplished, and explain that you offer them a great opportunity to share in those rewards. This is especially true if you work in a high-pressure environment, such as athletics or surgery. I always tell the kids I coach and my children that when someone says "I will be under a lot of pressure," they should immediately translate that into "I have been given a great opportunity." Pressure is opportunity for reward.

And all members of the team can share in those rewards—it doesn't have to be someone who does a job that we might traditionally consider primary. When the thoracic surgical division at UAB won the lowest-mortality award in 2012, I made a copy of the email notifying me that the team had won, and I had one of the men who clean our operating room come into my office. I sat down with him and read it to him. I spent four to five minutes talking to him about what this meant for our patients and us, and I thanked him for his hard work. His work helped reduce our infection rate, and he and his colleagues in the janitorial department share this award with us as much as any doctor or nurse. My patients were their patients as well. It is a team—united by a shared culture of enthusiasm.

Rub Some Dirt on It

In the summer of 1977, I turned fifteen years old and my dad told me I needed to get a real job. I vividly remember my first day on the job as a laborer at a New Jersey construction company. My fellow laborers were mostly in their twenties, looked and sounded quite different than me, and had been socialized in clearly very different circumstances. I wasn't sure exactly how this job was going to go for me.

I was grouped with three other laborers, and the very

first job we did started off at an old, dilapidated factory that engulfed an entire city block. Our job as laborers was to sweep the four city blocks that surrounded the factory. I got my broom and started sweeping. When I had finished my first street—at which point I was supposed to meet another of the laborers at the corner—I didn't see anybody else coming, so I just turned the corner and swept that street as well. I just kept going. Finally, when I got to the fourth and final street, I saw that all three of the other laborers were only halfway done with the first street they had started on—working as a team. Just then the foreman drove around and told me that everyone else was on a coffee break and that I needed to stop working and join them immediately. For about twenty minutes we did nothing but drink coffee and eat doughnuts while sitting inside the dilapidated building. A coffee break is something that I had never even heard of before.

I had never swept for that long or that hard, and over the course of the day I developed blisters. When the foreman saw that I was bleeding, he suggested that I go home. I was shocked. I told him that the injury was minor and that I would be fine. Finally I got my way and was able to finish out the shift as planned.

When my dad came home from work that night, I told him all about my day. I told him how inefficient the guys I worked with were, how many breaks we took, and how they really did not work that hard. I told him I could easily work with them;

in fact, I was working much harder than them. I told him, finally, how they wanted to send me home because of a few blisters. I remember him smiling to himself and chuckling.

Being able to play despite pain or injury is a lesson that lasts a lifetime and positions you to be a super performer, even if you have no special skill. Even after I became an attending thoracic surgeon and moved to Birmingham, Alabama, I liked to work outside and enjoyed some manual labor. Yard work around our house not only provided me some mental solace and time in the sun, but also gave me a chance to present the same opportunities to my three boys that my dad had given me when I was a child. Recently my boys and I removed thirty bushes from the front of our home. The job required a pick, axe, and shovels, as well as lots of work gloves. It was over a hundred degrees that entire weekend, without a cloud in the sky. My three boys and I took turns swinging the pick and axe and digging with the shovels. Despite having a baseball showcase in less than a week, Alec, my middle son, was too proud to stop, and he got terrible blisters from the pick. He did not want to let his teammates (his brothers or me) down. And that next weekend, he hit just fine—much as I've always operated just fine with blisters under my surgical gloves.

What I've learned, and what I've tried to teach my boys, is that it doesn't matter how difficult the problem may seem, or how much it may hurt to accomplish it. A commitment is a commitment, whether it is to your job, your patients, or even your Little League team. When you sign up for a team, any team, by definition you owe them your time, effort, and 100 percent commitment. You have to be at every game and every practice on time and ready to go.

I have head-coached or assistant-coached more than sixty Little League teams in baseball, basketball, football, and hockey over the past fifteen years for my three boys. One time I was coaching Alec in a seven-year-old basketball game. One of the boys on our team cut his finger, and he came running out of the game and showed it to me. It was a minor scratch—I can't even in good conscience label it a "cut"—so I told him it was nothing and that he should get back out on the floor, do his job, and compete. At this point, his mother came scurrying across the middle of the basketball court. Once she saw the blood (all two drops of it), she immediately took him out of the game and drove him to the emergency room. Alec was amazed. The culture that boy was raised in was obviously quite different from the one my wife and I created for our boys.

For example, when Matthew, my youngest son, was about six, he suffered a broken arm after falling from a jungle gym, after he had already signed up for baseball and soccer. He insisted on playing in his games anyway. And so—even though, yes, I know, he was only six—we let him play in his baseball and soccer games with a large cast on his arm. Matthew's friends still talk about it. It helped to define his culture.

We have great pictures of him standing triumphantly on third after he hit a triple—really just an infield ground ball—with one arm.

A mentality of toughness on the athletic field can translate to similar toughness later in life at whatever job you perform. No one exemplifies that attitude better than my dad.

After meals, my dad, who is a urologic surgeon, was having fevers and chills one week, as well as pain in the right upper quadrant of his abdomen. All of these are classic symptoms of an inflamed gallbladder—as he well knew. Yet he also knew that he had a large number of scheduled operations that week. My mom called me about his health problems, so I flew home the next day and went to his hospital, where I found him at work performing his scheduled operations. His temperature was 102 degrees, and I could see he was clearly septic, sick from infection. Within four hours, he found himself on the other end of the scalpel, having his gallbladder removed. The next morning, his nurse called my mom and told her that my father was missing from his hospital room. They eventually found him in the same hospital, two floors up, rounding on the patients he had operated on the day before. He was dragging around his own intravenous pole with him on rounds.

In order to be mentally tough, it helps to develop some level of physical toughness. Most of us work a sedentary job. We drive a car to work, take the elevator to our office, and barely break a sweat despite working eight to twelve hours a day. We may have worked hard all day, but we never get our heart rate above our baseline. In order to be successful, we have to be able to work through physical injuries such as back or joint pain or a minor flu. Working with some physical injuries helps promote mental agility and toughness. You do not have to be a martyr, but be honest with yourself and understand that most of the time, you can still do your job quite well even if you do not feel 100 percent.

Our culture has established too easily that it is okay to desire pain medicines and want paid time off from work. And once physicians name these ailments, we only escalate the problem by validating them. Obviously, some patients truly have physical afflictions, but many still go to work and endure the normal aches and pains of life and aging.

The idea of paid sick days seems counterproductive. I, like many people I know, have not missed a day of work due to illness in many years—seventeen in my case. I know of no one that I have infected by coming into work on days when I did not feel "perfect"—and my job is a lot more physically intimate than most. Although it does depend on the job one does, most people can avoid spreading infection by simply washing their hands and being careful about sharing objects like dishes or tools.

Thus, we should reward people for coming to work every day rather than pay them for assumed days out for illness. By providing bonuses to employees in your organization who have a perfect attendance record, you can help to create an expectation of physical and mental toughness that underlies a culture of super performance—a culture of honoring our commitments.

Striving to Hit .400 Every Year

My high school gave out an award each year to the best student athlete in each grade. I wrote down that I wanted to win the Klein Award in the ninth, tenth, and eleventh grades, and to win the most prestigious award at the senior graduation, the Deetjen Award. I accomplished most of these goals—and the key to accomplishing them was that I had written them down and placed the paper on my bedroom bureau in eighth grade, where for four years I could see it every night. By writing them down, I had made my goals clear and objective. You can do this too in work, sports, and life.

Goals are important, and they come in many different shapes, sizes, and types. And not all of them involve inanimate objects or awards. When I was a new surgical intern at Saint Francis Hospital in Hartford, Connecticut, in 1988, I was sitting with six surgical residents when the most beautiful woman I had ever seen in my life walked into the cafeteria. Every one of us turned around to watch her. She was blond, and there was a unique glow in her blue eyes. Everyone in the hospital knew her or of her. I asked my fellow residents her

story, and all of them said that she would not date any MDs—
especially surgeons.

And so another challenge or goal was made. I made a
goal—an overt, objective goal—to meet this woman and at
least to get to know her.

I still remember the first long conversation I had with
that nurse—Lorraine. It was a Thursday in September 1988.
We talked about life, our goals, about God, and about the family we wanted. I desired four kids, and she wanted three. The
result of that goal I set was that conversation that day—and,
eventually, twenty-two years of marriage and three teenage
boys. (Obviously, Lorraine got her way.)

Results can be just as important as goals. When I was
eighteen years old, I started playing semiprofessional baseball for the Elmwood Park Orioles in New Jersey. I played
shortstop. My goal was to hit at least .300 and to make fewer
than two errors in the entire year (a sixty-game season). To
achieve that goal, I recorded every part of every game: every
at bat, every pitch I saw, every playing chance I had in the
field, and every time I got on base.

It didn't take elaborate records for me to see that in that
year, I did not even come close to achieving my goals. I only
hit .272, and I made two errors in the first three games. My
dad reminds me (and quite often) that I had one game with
three errors in it by itself. Yet if I didn't have these records
of the performance—of the results of my goals—I wouldn't

have been able to improve that performance. The results can be just as important as the goals.

Goals and results should be a part of all super performers' lives, including surgeons. As a thoracic surgeon, one of the most common operations I perform is to remove part of the lung, called a "lobe," in patients who have developed lung cancer. I have now performed more than two thousand lobectomies, and my team and I track our surgical results daily. One way in which we do this is to print out records: diagrams that show the number of lobectomies we perform in a given period, as well as the complication and mortality rate for each of the five types of lobectomy.

One day, I told my youngest son, Matthew, who was about eight at the time, to go outside to our sports court and practice his left-handed basketball layups. At the time, Matthew was not very good with his left hand, and other teams were exposing this weakness and pushing him left. So I told him to work on this technique by recording how many layups he made and how many he missed.

After Matthew came in from being outside for a while, dripping with sweat, he noticed one of my lobectomy result diagrams on the kitchen table. As he drank his iced tea, he studied the figure and noted that I had a higher complication rate for right-lower lobectomies than I did for the other four types of lobectomies listed. He said, "Dad, forget me practicing my left-handed layups. That's just basketball. You better go back to the hospital today and practice your right-lower lobectomies; you are not very good at them, and you need to get better."

Setting Specific, Measurable Goals

Results are not only important to goals; results *define* goals. Every individual should have clear goals that are objective and measurable. Goals such as "to be happy," "to do well at work," or "to get along" are too nebulous and esoteric. How can you possibly measure whether you're happier today than yesterday? To be successful, you have to be able to define your goals by measurable results.

In addition, we are all team members in one way or another. Even professional golfers and single tennis players are part of a larger team, something bigger than just themselves. Thus we should all have clear goals for our team as well. Last year, my team's goal was to do more thoracic operations than anybody else in the world and to have the lowest mortality and the highest patient satisfaction. We achieved the first, but not the second or third. But we are close, and our focus on tracking our results helps us to know *how* close.

Often, our team goals and our individual goals should relate to one another. For example, it is not selfish for Tom Brady to desire to win the most-valuable-player award and to have the highest quarterback rating in the NFL this year, because neither of these things could happen unless his team is playing well overall (at least on the offensive side of the ball). In order to achieve his individual goal, he has to achieve his team goals as well (such as winning the Super Bowl).

To achieve team goals, team members should hold one another accountable in order to ensure that they are all aligned with one another's individual goals, as well as with the overall team or family goals. (Companies can do this on a hierarchical level, but then need to break it down into their divisions or departments and do it there as well.)

Too often, athletes enter an arena or professionals enter their place of business without a clear-cut goal for themselves or for their organization on that particular day or for that year. I see this commonly in the gym, when an athlete is walking around randomly going from one exercise machine to another instead of following a clear plan with clearly tracked results. Instead—and in all areas of life—we should show foresight in our goal setting and have the prudence, as well as the mental and physical toughness, to change our behavior in order to maximize the chances of achieving our goals.

Find the High Ground

When I was thirteen years old, I decided that I wanted to be a surgeon when I grew up. This epiphany occurred when my dad decided to spay our family dog in our basement. I recall him studying up on how to deliver the anesthesia and how best to position the dog. It was an area he operated in every day in humans, and the anatomy is almost exactly the same. Since he had spayed dogs in the lab when he was a surgical resident, and since he loved our dog, he wanted to do it himself to make sure it was done right. He let me and the whole family assist him in the operation. I suspect that not too many children—not even the children of surgeons—get this experience. But once I saw the incredible insides of a living creature, my life was changed forever. I had never thought of my dad—a man whom I loved and adored—as someone who was skilled enough to do that type of operation, especially for our beloved dog. I just knew him as my dad. But what he could do was amazing, magnificent. One day, I wanted to be able to do what he did.

About one week later, a neighbor noticed our beagle out for a walk and remarked on how good the stitching looked on the incision. He asked us who had performed the operation. I waited for my dad proudly to take the credit. Instead, he just said it had been "a veterinarian he knew well."

He was always modest and quiet. He was not only modest about his own accomplishments but also about his children's, even if they performed well in a baseball game.

That same year, I played an all-star game in New Jersey. I pitched the whole game, threw a one-hitter, and went 3–4 at the plate with four RBIs. At the end of the game, I walked across the field to approach my dad. He had been talking to two men the entire game. One man was about seventy-five and the other was about forty years old. Given my performance, I was pretty sure that they must have been talking about what a stud I was. My father introduced me to the two men, who were father and son. The older man said that my dad had operated on him a few years earlier and had removed his cancerous prostate gland. My dad had saved his life. They were both there to watch the first baseman of the team I had played, who was their grandson and son, respectively.

The older man said, upon shaking my hand: "Nice game, son. What position did you play?"

I was amazed: Apparently my father hadn't mentioned that I was the starting pitcher or hitting third in the lineup in the game that all three of them had come to see.

Not only did my father's modesty become clearer to me that day, but the importance of what he did as a surgeon did as well. The two men weren't impressed by me but rather by my dad: The removal of the older man's cancer had been a lot more important than my baseball game. Everywhere we went, people knew my mom (who was my dad's head nurse in his office) and my dad, and they often thanked them for all they did.

I was becoming further and further convinced that medicine—and especially surgery—was for me. Seeing the skill of which my dad was capable, the essential modesty of the work he did, and the way he made an active, powerful difference in people's lives: It felt like the highest calling I could aspire to.

And it still does. About one month ago, I received an urgent call from an outstanding surgeon who was operating just two floors above me. He needed an extra set of hands. I was in the middle of an operation of my own, but I was honored to be able to rush up there to help. The surgeon was attempting to cut out a large tumor from an elderly man. The cancer was big and growing into large arteries and veins deep in this obese patient's pelvis and groin. The patient was in trouble, and he was receiving a blood transfusion when I arrived. This surgeon was extremely experienced and technically outstanding, and he only needed another set of experienced hands to complete the complicated operation. Together, we were able to sew up the bleeding vessels, remove the tumor, and get the patient safely off of the operating-room table. As I walked out of that operating room that day I had an incredible feeling of value. Perhaps I was finally living up to that higher calling, at least for that moment.

In anything you do, find the high ground: Aspire to live up to the noblest, highest aspect of your job. Certain jobs—such as police work, firefighting, teaching, or working in health care—are essentially service oriented, which makes the nobility part easy since the job lends itself to this action. However, even less overtly service-oriented jobs can still provide the feeling of fulfillment and satisfaction of community service. Many entertainers, professional athletes, or those who work in the financial sector find this high ground. For example, many actors and wealthy businesspeople have set up foundations that provide an incredible array of services to needy people in the community, and many pro athletes use the platform that their athletic talent and money provide to make a difference in many other people's lives. Even though they may "just hit a baseball" and even though some fail to see the redeeming societal value of this, there can be a lot.

But you do not have to be a surgeon or Derek Jeter or the CEO of Ford—all of us can do it in a small way. We can be honest at work, and we can find community service that we can perform in our jobs or in our local areas. Many people who can't afford to give money give their time. Many people find ways to take assignments at work that dovetail well with personal goals. All of us can find the high ground in our work and lives.

Be the Go-To Guy

During tight games, I have noticed how many team members get up and cheer and rally for one another. This attitude is admirable—the players know that this is the critical moment, and thus they all want to come together. But somebody has to step up and be willing to take the last-second shot. Somebody has to be willing to try in the critical moment and risk failure. Somebody has to be willing to be called the goat in order to one day be called the hero. This person is the "go-to guy."

Being the go-to guy doesn't guarantee success. If you're the go-to guy, they may call you into the operating room to help stop a patient from bleeding to death, and you may fail; the patient may not survive. But you were known as the one willing to take the risk; you were the one in the arena. You were the go-to guy—which meant that people knew they could rely on you.

It takes time and practice to become the go-to guy. Part of it, of course, is the confidence to want the ball in a critical situation, but confidence that is not supported by skills that have been honed by hours of practice is foolish hubris. Most importantly, however, if you miss that shot and your team loses one night, the go-to guy is not afraid to do it again the next night. If your business or organization is in trouble but you have put the time into your organization, worked your way up from the bottom rung, and truly understand how the organization works, you cannot be afraid to speak your mind and offer your suggestions.

I have always been a fan of famous quotes and have collected many of them over the years. But I have only one quote that is framed in my university office. It is by Theodore Roosevelt, who said:

> It is not the critic who counts; not the man who points out how the strong man stumbles, or where the doer of deeds could have done better. The credit belongs to the man who is actually in the arena, whose face is marred by dust and sweat and blood; who strives valiantly; who errs, who comes short again and again, because there is no effort without error and shortcoming; but who does actually strive to do the deeds; who

knows great enthusiasms, the great devotions; who spends himself in a worthy cause; who at the best knows in the end the triumph of high achievement, and who at the worst, if he fails, at least fails while daring greatly, so that his place shall never be with those cold and timid souls who neither know victory nor defeat.

CHAPTER 2

Enjoy the Long Bus Rides

Riding the Escalator of Life

. . .

Performing When the Spotlight Is Brightest

Fueling the Internal Flame of a Super Performer

Recently, in a lecture I gave as a visiting professor, one of my slides contained two pictures: an elevator and an escalator. The import of the slide was that too many of us view our lives as rides on an elevator. We see ourselves as traveling from one floor to another with only finite, predefined stops where we can get off and walk around. These stops are predetermined: high school graduation, college graduation, getting married, a week-long vacation to your beach house where you can "finally relax." Apart from those stops on the elevator, we are immersed in our work and our lives, confined in a small box-like compartment that prevents us from looking around.

But life isn't like an elevator, and these stops do not represent our only opportunities to enjoy life. I often hear people say, "I can't wait for next week when I get to go on vacation." Why does life only start next week? What about today?

Life should be more like a ride on an escalator: a gradual rise upward. There is always the opportunity to enjoy the beautiful panoramic view. Opportunities abound at all times, and the road to success is long and continuous rather than just a series of stages.

The road to success in medicine is unusually long and painful. In cardiothoracic surgery, it involves a sixteen-year apprenticeship. After I finished my four years of college, four years of medical school, my five years of general surgical training (with every other night on call), and my three years of cardiothoracic training, I was thirty-four years old. Only then was I finally done with my training and ready to start my professional career.

I got my first real job as an attending cardiothoracic surgeon at the University of Alabama at Birmingham. One of my friends, with whom I played high school football, had just retired from his nine-year NFL career. He already had his Super Bowl ring; my professional career was just starting.

And, of course, that didn't feel great. But too many people see these necessary years of maturation as wasted steps that delay their ultimate gratification. Many literally count them down, day by day, almost like a prison sentence.

Recently I was a visiting professor at a major university. Before my lecture, one of the thoracic fellows who was giving me a tour of the hospital showed me a countdown he kept running on his iPhone. It read: 1 year, 228 days, and some odd hours and minutes to go. It was the time he had left in his cardiothoracic residency program.

What did he expect to happen when the countdown ran out? The reality is that when a phase of your life ends—when the elevator reaches its floor—nothing magical changes in you or in your life. It's true that your salary goes up, but so will your bills. As a resident, when there's sudden bleeding in the operating room, there's often a senior doctor on hand to bail you out; once you are the attending surgeon and on the next "floor," there is no one else to bail you out of trouble. And after you have been promoted to boss, you may miss the days when you were only responsible for your own sales figures and not those of an entire division. The next phase of your life may not be as great as you think.

Alec, my middle son, was getting close to high school graduation. One of his friends was telling me how lame high school was and how he could not wait for it to end and for college to start. Alec laughed; he knew what speech was coming. I explained to his friend that I had just heard the same thing from the college student who shadowed me, the medical student the day before that, the general surgical resident

41

last week, and the cardiothoracic fellow who operated with me yesterday. If you see your life as an elevator, stuck in some box and waiting for the doors to open on the next floor, then you're not going to be satisfied with where you are, maybe ever. And that's something that won't change, no matter how high the floor you've reached might be.

What's more, those years of training are necessary for any professional to create a base and form a process. There are both emotional and physical aspects that go into it. Respect the necessity of those years. Spend the time enjoying that maturation process, and learn from it. Try to learn everything you can so that when you are under pressure, you have properly prepared.

Training isn't a prison sentence that prevents you from living life *now*. Life is an ongoing process of learning and getting better, of adapting as you age and as the environment around you constantly changes. So enjoy the entire gradual escalator ride.

Enjoy each phase of life. Write down the positive aspects of this phase of life that you might not have in the next phase. Capitalize on opportunities you have now that you will not have in the next stage. Do not wish so hard for one to end and the next to start. Each phase has its unique advantages and disadvantages. Respect the process of aging and learning. Don't just stumble onto the silver lining in the bad phases; actively seek them out. Allow the process to occur—and be smart enough to realize that as you age, you will necessarily look back at many of those stages and be envious that you are not back there reliving them now.

Iverson Got It All Wrong

Allen Iverson was a ten-time all-star in the NBA and a rookie of the year and league MVP in 2001, but he is unfortunately best known now for his infamous, inarticulate monologue about his views on practice. If you are one of the few people in the world who has not heard the interview, you should watch it on YouTube. In it, Iverson responds to a question about whether or not he missed a practice with the following: "Come on, man . . . we're talking about practice . . . not a game . . . not a game . . . but practice. . . . How am I going to make my teammates better during practice?"

I've always thought it's interesting that we describe ourselves as "practicing" medicine. The whole reason we call it practicing medicine is because even when a surgery (or any procedure) is finished, you—the practitioner—are never done with training or learning ways to get better. As long as you are caring for sick patients, you are always in the learning phase. The patients see to that.

As a thoracic surgeon, I do robotic lung surgery. This means I operate while sitting down and looking into a console that is fifteen feet or sometimes even farther away from the patient.

In other words, unlike traditional surgery, I am not standing at the patient's bedside. This physical distance or separation from the patient makes many surgeons very anxious, especially thoracic surgeons. Instead, the patient is prepared on the operating-room table. We make several small incisions so that we can place small instruments and a high-definition camera in the chest. Next we attach the robotic arms to these instruments, and then we sit down at the console. As we move our hands, the robot mimics our movements and moves the instruments inside the patient's chest cavity. This allows us to do the same operation, but through very small incisions and with great precision.

During a robotic lobectomy, we remove a part of a patient's lung, called a lobe. The surgeon and her team have to carefully navigate around small branches coming from the pulmonary artery (which carries blood from the heart to the lungs). These arterial branches can be very large or very small, but they carry a large amount of blood, and they're always extremely thin-walled—sometimes only a few millimeters in size—which means they have to be controlled (ligated, tied, sewn, or stapled closed) so that they do not bleed.

Princess Diana of Wales died in the bowels of the Pont de l'Alma road tunnel in Paris when her pulmonary artery was torn during her high-speed car accident. But even in the operating room, a tear in this artery can be fatal. And a tear can occur in an instant. It is the most feared and devastating intraoperative complication that a general thoracic surgeon can encounter.

Several weeks ago, in front of three visiting surgeons, my team encountered it. We had a tear in the patient's pulmonary artery. However, our team had practiced our response to this many times, and we went into autopilot because of our preparation. According to our safety protocol, I had placed a sponge in the chest right next to the artery, and I quickly grabbed the sponge with one of the robotic arms and applied pressure to the bleeding vessel. My bedside assistant, a critical member of our team, handed me another sponge in under three seconds. Her quick and calm moves helped to stop the bleeding and save the patient's life.

Since this event, I have watched this videotape many times, both alone and with my operative team. We watched it to time our response, to see what we did well, and to think about what we could have done better and how we might have been able to prevent the tear in the first place.

Every time I watch this video, one fact becomes clearer and clearer: Allen Iverson got it all wrong. It *is* all about practice, and you *do* make your teammates better by practicing. The positive outcome in this situation only occurred because my team, like most surgical teams, had prepared for this event many times. Practice hones the team's skill and ability to react under pressure, and it prepares a team for when things are going wrong. The preparation during the practice was the key to the successful outcome, and during practice, we all made each other better.

Forming Good Practice Habits

Good practice habits cannot start off young enough. Many parents laughed at me when I mailed out the ten-minute breakdown of my one-hour ice-hockey practice for my team of five-year-olds. We only got the ice for an hour each week, so we had to be very efficient. The kids went from station to station so that they did not get bored. No one was ever in a line, and they were skating the entire time. This maximized ice time and minimized their chance of getting disinterested, which I learned happens quickly and often at that age. Moreover, we made the kids responsible for being on time. If they were late for more than two practices or games, they could not start the game, and they had to miss a shift. There is nothing better than watching a five- or six-year-old kid jump out of a car and tell mommy and daddy, "Hurry up, or Coach Cerfolio is going to bench me!"

But however often you can "get the ice" to practice, so to speak, it's important to structure your practices to allow for similar efficiency. Many members of a team do not fully understand the purpose of team practice or their roles during team-practice time. Individuals have to work on honing their skills, but much of that can be done during individual practice time. The goal of a team practice is to use every second the team is together to maximize the team's chance to win.

During most games, business deals, or other events, things can and will go wrong. There are ebbs and flows and momentum shifts in surgery just as there are in sporting events or business meetings. The team needs to mentally prepare for these scenarios with both physical and mental agility and to have predetermined responses to negative events.

For example: In my Little League baseball practices, I intentionally put my infielders under pressure by telling them they could not go home until we, as a team, made nine plays in a row without an error. This allowed me to see how the players reacted to those errors as a team. When we discuss the error immediately afterward, the focus is on everyone's response to the error, not on the error itself. We review our reactions and go over how we can better respond to errors of that kind as a team.

That's fundamental to practice: Each team member should be able to prepare a response to every scenario in which something goes wrong. In addition, it's a good idea to write down a list of those situations where something goes wrong, along with the mental and physical response used to counter each type of error. (You can, and should, practice your emotional response to negative events, just as you practice your physical response—just as we do it in the operating room.) Preparing for these events—and establishing guidelines within your organization for how employees should react in certain crisis situations—makes the team's response better. It *is* all about team practice.

Hubris Hurts

Confidence is good. It provides comfort under pressure. But too much confidence can hurt you.

When my oldest son, Robby, was seven, he played in his first year of kid-pitch baseball. Although he was only seven, he played with eight-year-olds, and well enough to be named an all-star the day before his championship game. In the last inning of that game, it seemed as if Robby's team was the clear winner: There were two outs with men on first and second, and Robby's team was ahead by one. Even better: Robby was about to face one of the other team's worst hitters, a boy who had struck out his last time up. Robby and I were confident that he would strike him out again, and so I called for an 0–2 fastball right down the middle. The kid hit a line-drive base hit up the middle, and our center fielder let it go through his legs. It rolled to the fence, and both runners scored. We lost that game, and that hit—which Robby had been confident would be yet another strikeout—was the game changer.

The lesson was clear: Never underestimate an opponent. This lesson not only applies to small, unassuming athletes, but also to small, noninvasive cancers.

It should have been an easy, straightforward operation. The computed tomographic (CT) scan of the chest showed a small two-centimeter tumor in the right-lower lobe, and I had done over fifteen hundred lobectomies by this time: What was one more, especially with a tumor this small? We had two visiting surgeons watching us this day, as we frequently do.

We had completed seven operations already, and this was our last operation of the day. Just like Robby's game, it should have been an easy win.

But during the operation, I put a hole in the pulmonary artery. It was a big laceration, one that caused a lot of bleeding and much anxiety to everyone in the operating room. We fixed it and the patient did fine. But again the teaching point was clear: Never underestimate the opponent, whether it's in surgery, sports, or in life.

One of my European visitors had another way of saying this, commenting on the operation as I was closing: "In my country we have a saying: There are snakes behind every bush, and even the smallest one can deliver a lethal bite."

Professionals do not have mental lapses, and they do not prepare less for an apparently weaker opponent than they do for a more obviously challenging one. Your preparation before what may seem like a slam-dunk easy win should be the same as it is before the championship game. In fact, if it is, you'll be less nervous and less likely to underperform during the championship game. The mental and physical preparation required before each meeting or before closing any deal should be the same. This routine provides comfort before the big game. Take no victory for granted.

Make no mistake: I don't mean you shouldn't have confidence. As athletes, performers, and successful businesspeople—as competitors in any field—confidence is important. And most of us have received accolades or awards, or maybe even special degrees, for our success. These awards help to form the pillars and fabric of our confidence. In other words: It is only human nature to think, sometimes, that you really are as good as people tell you. And if you do believe that, it follows that you can take a break from your preparation.

But it's a mistake to believe the hype. Because the reality is that the competition is always coming, and they will catch you. I frequently tell the residents that every day, the tumors we'll have to operate on are getting bigger, and the patients are getting older, sicker, and weaker.

No matter how many awards you've won or how much success you've had, it's a fact that every day, your opponents are catching up on you. Reputations do not win games. The cancer does not jump out of the patient's chest because it's heard that we have one of the busiest and best thoracic-surgical cancer centers in the world. We have to go out and perform and execute under pressure. We have to dissect out the arteries and veins and ligate them without bleeding—even for small cancers—every day, day after day, several times a day. The opponents are never going to give it away, irrespective of their shape, size, or the odds against them.

Remind yourself of that every time someone tells you how good you are. Remind yourself that there are younger, smarter, faster, and more motivated competitors on the way, and while you are navel-gazing and reading your press clippings again, they are getting better.

It is okay to cut out your newspaper clippings. In fact, it

is good to do so. I recommend it—it's one of the major "lines of gratification" we talked about in chapter 1. But just as staring again and again at the marks the lawnmower made in your lawn won't stop the next crop of grass from growing or help you prepare to cut it, reading your press clippings over and over again—unless you're very depressed or closing in on retirement—is not going to help you perform. Rereading your own favorable press clippings plays no role in your pregame preparation. So do cut out your clippings, read them once, and store them in a safe, remote space where you rarely look. After all, you may need them later in life for your retirement party—or perhaps for a roast at your expense. (After all, remember that as quickly as our society loves to create role models, we love to tear them down even more quickly.)

Ignite the Internal and Eternal Flame

Some people know exactly what drives them—their "internal flame"—but I am amazed at how many do not. For me, it all goes back to one afternoon.

When I was in the seventh grade, I came home one day from school and saw my parents extremely upset. They were both sobbing and holding one another in our formal living room, a room we only went into on Christmas Eve and Thanksgiving. I had never seen my mom or dad so visibly hurt—and before that day, I had never seen my father cry.

I believed then and still believe now that I have the greatest parents in the world. They were always there for us, and they dedicated their lives to teaching us about life's lessons—including, as you've seen throughout this chapter, inculcating a work ethic and a value system that would last us for the rest of our lives. I couldn't imagine what could have happened to make them this visibly and emotionally upset. That day I found out that my brother had gotten in serious trouble at school.

I remember making a lifelong promise that day, that very afternoon, that I would never do anything to hurt my parents. I made a determination not to fail. I would do what I needed to do to make them proud of me and my actions and ensure that they were never upset or injured by me. This has been my internal flame—an attitude that has given me fuel for a lifetime.

To help yourself be the best, you should find your own internal flame. Think about what fuels you. It's not a matter of hypnosis or childhood regression: The answer, in some way, should be obvious. What makes you get up early each morning and work hard? Is it your family, your children, your parents? Is it for you?

Once you have your answer, write it down. If you find it awkward to write it down, then you should openly discuss it with your family members or team members at work. Find some way to articulate it, to make it more tangible.

Once you've articulated it—once you know exactly what it is—you can make that flame grow stronger and last longer.

Too often, our goals or desires are not strong enough to

sustain the continued behavioral change that is fully required to achieve the long-term goals. The desire is often gone after a few short weeks. So it's important to figure out how to keep the flame burning—not so high that it burns you out completely, but high enough to daily fuel you to be great.

After writing down your internal flame, under it write down specific ways you can keep that flame burning for long periods of time. Be specific about how you will maintain this passion and what steps you can take—both as a person and as an organization—to maintain it.

Since we all change over time, as does our competition, we must evolve. Our motivation must evolve as we do. Before I had children, my internal flame was mostly about me, my development, and my success. After I got married, it was more about my wife and me, and then after my three boys were born, it became mostly about my children and helping to ensure their success.

It amazes me that although so many people take time every year (or even twice a year) to reevaluate their stock portfolios and retirement plans and to enact changes, so few people do this when it comes to their own personal goals. Few of us review the promises that we must all make to our families or identify the group or individuals who motivate us. Just like our financial portfolios, we need to rebalance and retool our sources of motivation regularly.

Therefore, once you've written down or otherwise articulated your internal flame and your specific plan for keeping it burning, review that plan every three to six months with other team members or family members as well. Taking questions of personal motivation as seriously as we take our finances provides us with a specific technique that forces us to reevaluate ourselves every quarter as individuals and as an organization. It prevents us from being static and inflexible, and it forces us to be adaptable and to evolve with the changing circumstances we are all faced with every day in our families, our jobs, and our lives.

Always Choose the Highest Peak

I was sure I wanted to be a surgeon when I first went to medical school, but I did not know what type. As a third-year medical student, I possessed few clinical skills and thus—like most other third-year medical students—was of little help to the resident doctors in the hospital. However, I still had to take in every aspect of the hospital in order to learn how it all worked.

One night in 1986, at three thirty a.m., I was woken from a deep sleep by the blare of the code pager. By the time I got to the code, there were already nine people in the patient's room. Doctors were taking turns doing chest compressions and CPR on an obese elderly man whose heart had stopped. Contradictory orders were being shouted left and right, and many of us, though trying to help, were interfering with one another. It was pure bedlam in that room.

That is, it was pure bedlam until a senior cardiothoracic

fellow strolled in. He immediately took control of the code. He told people to shut up, and he asked those who were non-essential to the patient's care to leave (so I hid in the back). After speaking to the senior medical resident, the fellow took a long needle and carefully slipped it into the left side of the patient's chest. The needle slowly filled with blood from the pericardial space—blood that was preventing the patient's heart from pumping normally—and the patient's heart rate and blood pressure slowly returned to normal. The patient was back—he was alive. The surgeon asked if he could go back to bed, and he left.

This was one of the first incidents that made me consider cardiothoracic surgery as a career. I had always heard that cardiothoracic surgeons had the hardest training and that only the best and the brightest could get in and survive. The more I thought about it, the more the idea of it appealed to me. Maybe this was the peak I was to climb.

Why was this my instinct—to follow the hardest path that I could find within the field of surgery? Again, I trace it back to upbringing. Finding the highest and hardest peak to climb can be taught early in one's life—especially through sports—and when it came to raising my own children, I tried to pass on the same lesson.

By the time my youngest son, Matthew, started to play basketball at age five, I had already coached at least eight basketball teams with Robby and Alec, and I knew what we needed to do to be successful. We scouted and filmed other teams, and we knew all of their plays. We filmed all of our games and had video sessions every week. But after winning every game for three straight seasons, I knew that Matthew, the team, and I all needed a higher challenge.

Thus we entered the public-school league, which had 144 kids competing at each grade level (as opposed to only 19 boys in our normal basketball league.) The teams we competed against actually had tryouts; they were not just a sign-up league like we had played in. We did not do quite so well at first and only played .500 ball—won half our games, lost half. We weren't used to losing. But we knew we had to raise the bar, and that meant we had to learn how to lose as well. The only way we would get better was to raise the level of the competition, to try to ascend a higher mountain.

Success begets more success. However, if one is stagnant and is happy beating weaker opponents, if one doesn't actively seek out the best competition, then those victories and successes are empty. You have to always choose the highest peak to climb.

If you are the CEO of a company, you should incentivize your team members to want to beat the best. If you are a coach and you have a team that is dominating at a certain level, you have to buy into the concept that it is best for the kids to go to the next level. This means you will have to accept some losses early on, but it may be a necessary step for you and your team to grow. Actively seek out the best and compete against them. As I've shown, this is true for our children as well. If you have a child that is dominating in a sport, move them up to an older age group so that they can compete against older kids. (Some people suggest travel leagues, but these tend to be expensive and disruptive to the family, and in my experience they waste a lot of time.)

In sports, the idea of choosing to compete against the strongest competition you can find is an easy concept and model. However, in the business world, the stakes are higher and it can be more difficult. If you are profitable in what you are doing, it is not always prudent to enter a more competitive market or to diversify into other areas. But ultimately, as a competitor you have to want to beat the best, and if no one is close, you have to push yourself to get better. The only difference is the amount of prudence and preparation you require before beginning the new climb.

Prudence is important because super performance does not always lead to super success. Just because you worked really hard, prepared perfectly, and executed your plans just right does not mean that you will win the game, make the deal, win the big contract, or save the patient's life. Sometimes the outcome is bad.

However, although performance doesn't always lead to success, a commitment to process improvement *always* leads to success. The problem is that too many are unwilling to perform critical analysis on their process. Too often, when we lose, we conclude, "We were unlucky, we could not have prepared any better, we could not have tried any harder." Very rarely are these statements true. Losing is a part of the process, but you can always work harder, prepare better, or start preparing sooner.

After a devastating loss, it's good to take some time to heal. But within twenty-four hours you must start to critically review why you lost. Do not be too quick to conclude that there was nothing else you could have done, and don't limit your review to the immediate situation. Too many coaches just review the tape of the game they lost. Sometimes, the reason for the loss occurred long before the game started. Review each and every process you and your team used to prepare for your challenge. Review the physical and mental aspects of the pregame anxiety management; even review your meals and lodging. Be bold enough and honest enough to challenge your organization's processes or systems, even after a win. Always strive to make the process better, faster, more efficient, and less costly. It is the commitment to process improvement that defines you and your team, not just your win/loss record.

It Ain't Over Until the Fat Lady Sings

Despite my experience with cardiothoracic surgery in my third year of medical school and my thoughts in that direction, I wasn't yet 100 percent convinced, and for a while I followed an alternate path. During my fourth year of medical school, I decided to follow in my father's footsteps and be a urologic surgeon. Initially, I wanted to go to the number-one-ranked program in the country—the New York Hospital–Cornell and Memorial Sloan Kettering Cancer Center in New York City—and I got accepted there. However, in order to be a urologist (urologic surgeon), you have to do two years of general surgery, and once I learned that residents in New York didn't get many chances to operate during those first two years, I decided to perform my first two years of general surgical training elsewhere. I applied to a smaller program in Hartford, Connecticut—Saint Francis Hospital. I was incredibly lucky and received my first choice in both matches, so I went off to Hartford, to be a general surgeon-in-training for two years.

It was at Saint Francis that the most important and meaningful event in my life happened: I met my wife-to-be, Lorraine B. Mojcik, RN, as described in the previous chapter. But another highly meaningful event occurred while I was in Hartford: After seeing several amazing thoracic surgeons and after seeing what they could do inside a patient's chest, I realized that thoracic surgery was for me after all. So I decided to switch career paths.

But I had a problem, because I did not have a job in thoracic surgery. I needed to complete three more years of general surgical training and then three years of cardiothoracic surgical training. I did not want to move again during that training, so I wanted to start off in the best place for thoracic surgery: the Mayo Clinic.

The first time I called David Nagorney, the head of the Mayo Clinic residency training program, about joining him, he very nicely explained to me over the phone that he did not have any positions in his general surgical program for me at the time. He wished me good luck—in other words, he was telling me I had lost.

But I was not going away that easily. I prepared diligently and called his secretary every day for the next two weeks before I finally got through to him. The next time I spoke to him, my preparation paid off, and I got him to agree to at least interview me. I flew up to Rochester, Minnesota, on a Thursday, and after five interviews I had a job there for the next six years.

Although I was in a desperate situation, I never gave up. Somehow, I was blessed with this new, incredible opportunity. And because of that, I had to confront one of my first major experiences with failure.

During your second year of cardiothoracic fellowship training, part of your duties involve going through a congenital heart rotation: operating on young children and newborns who are born with abnormal hearts. The stakes of these operations are high.

One day in clinic, we met a beautiful blond five-year-old boy named Dylan. Dylan's parents were young, good looking, and smart, and they loved each other and their other two children. But Dylan was smaller and weaker than the others. Dylan was dying from congenital heart disease. We operated on him the next day, replacing two faulty heart valves and rerouting the blood in his heart. He had a flawless operation performed by one of the best congenital heart surgeons in the world. The execution could not have been better.

Dylan did great for a few days, and his parents were gracious and thankful. He was out of the intensive care unit, on the floor and walking and eating, and all of his tubes were out. He was one day away from going home.

At two a.m., the nurse called me urgently. Dylan had coded; his heart had stopped. I was sleeping in a call room thirty feet down the hall and I came running. His father was yelling for us to do something, and his mother was sobbing in the corner of the room in her bedside cot. They were escorted to a waiting area. I quickly intubated Dylan and then reopened his chest with a knife and wire cutters. I spread his tiny sternum apart. The heart looked lifeless. It was distended and blue and firm and not moving.

I started doing cardiac massage and called for backup. I gave him multiple rounds of every medicine we had. But his heart did not respond. I kept working. I continued to do cardiac compressions. But his heart remained lifeless. There was no cardiac rhythm, no blood pressure.

As I kept going—as the minutes passed away—I knew that I could not quit. I could not fail this child or this family. This family and kid were too perfect; they deserved better; Dylan deserved better. He could not die. He was not going to die on my watch.

"Give him another round of epi!" I barked at the nurse. She shook her head in disapproval, but she gave him another dose. I was not going to call it. My arms and legs were aching from the CPR over the past two hours, and I remember sweating so profusely that they had to keep wiping my face so that I didn't drip my sweat into his chest.

Two hours and fifteen minutes after the code started, the attending surgeon came in. The nurses had called him some time ago and told him what was happening. I was soaked in sweat and exhausted, but the code was still going. I had not called it. The attending surgeon tapped me on the shoulder and whispered in my ear: "Robert, Dylan is dead. You have to stop."

I should have called the code sooner, the nurses said, and they were right: I should have. But I just did not want to quit—not on this kid, not on Dylan. I remember looking at his blue, swollen face: His eyes were still so bright, but lifeless. Dylan was dead, so I called it.

Then the attending surgeon had me do something that I will never forget. He had me go out first, to be the one who told Dylan's parents that Dylan had died. He knew I needed to learn how to do this, how to admit defeat and face up to the fact that we had lost. It was an incredible lesson I learned that day from a world-class surgeon and from Dylan. I will never forget either one of them.

About fifteen years later I was invited to come back to where I had trained and to serve as a visiting professor at the Mayo Clinic. At the end of one of my lectures, a middle-aged nurse came up to me. I did not recognize her. She told me that she was present on the night of Dylan's code. She was a young nursing student then. She wanted to talk to me about that night fifteen years before. She told me it was the first cardiac arrest she had ever been to, and she thought that they would all last two hours. Since then, she has been involved in hundreds of codes and has learned that most are only fifteen to twenty minutes, and rarely do the patients survive.

She said that although the outcome was devastating, our attitude of never giving up had inspired her. We talked for some time about that night with Dylan, about that beautiful family, and about the many lessons they had taught us that night and every day afterward.

Chief among these, whatever the outcome had been: Never give up, even when a situation seems incredibly desperate. Never give up, even when some things seem impossible. In 2012, the San Francisco Giants proved that in baseball countless times. Many corporations have come back from bankruptcy and Chapter 11 to thrive again.

Yes, it is true that sometimes you have to know when the competition is over and face the music of the loss. When loss is inevitable, finish the event with dignity and grace and learn from it. Seasoned professionals know when to keep fighting and when to stop and admit defeat with grace. But if you are not sure—or if there is any flicker of hope—keep fighting to the end.

The best way to foster an attitude of never quitting is to teach it early in one's life. During team scrimmages, I would often intentionally pick on one team over another. I would put one team down a lot, or give them purposely bad calls, just to see how the players would react. By learning not to give up even when the situation was deliberately unfair, they learned the concept of never giving up for a lifetime.

Many people never learn this, but you can help to teach them. A "never-quit attitude" has to be a culture, not a motto, and it must be slowly infused from the management downward. Once, in a Little League baseball game where we won in the last inning when we were down 7–0, I told my kids that we just needed one runner on base. If we got just one runner, and if we could get into their bullpen, we would win this game. The second batter of that inning walked after our first struck out. When their coach made a pitching change, I told my kids we were going to win. Because they believed me, we did.

Shining When the Lights Are Bright

Robby and I walked off the baseball field for the last time before his first college baseball showcase. We had practiced all facets of his game: defense, hitting, sliding, and pitching. This was to be his moment to shine or to choke, his coming-out party or his going-away party. It was a critical opportunity to peak at the right time and perform under pressure.

I could not go—I had to work—but I remember getting the call from Lorraine as Robby walked to the mound for the first time. At first, there were only six or seven scouts behind the fence with radar guns. After he struck out the first three batters, Lorraine told me that more and more began to make their way over to the field. He faced ten batters that day and struck out eight, ten up and ten down. By the end of the day, he had multiple offers from several excellent Division One baseball schools.

Robby succeeded because he knew this day would be critical to his future. He understood the opportunity. And so he prepared for months—years, really—and he delivered several great performances when the lights were brightest.

Operating-room lights are just like the stadium lights of a baseball field. They are hot, intense, and cast an incredible amount of attention on a very small part of the world. There is no hiding your performance under the white-hot, discerning eyes of these lights. Everyone can see your performance.

Sometimes the lights on a certain situation are more intense than others. One common piece of advice I give a surgeon who is about to start his or her career is to avoid having a high-profile death early in their career. Any death of any patient is obviously bad, but high-profile deaths include preventable deaths, the death of any patient who was a beloved hospital employee, or the death of a young child. Obviously, all of these are remembered far longer than "ordinary" deaths, and the risk to a budding surgeon's career is considerable. But sometimes, it's necessary to take the risk.

When I was at UAB for only about nine months, I accepted the transfer of a newborn baby from Texas. Her name was Anna. Both her parents were physicians and the mother was a surgeon, and Anna was only forty-eight hours old. Anna was dying because she was born with a congenital abnormality of her trachea (windpipe) called tracheal stenosis. A long segment of her trachea was critically narrowed, extending below her neck and into the segment behind her heart. Because of this abnormality, she was unable to breathe, even on a ventilator. She would not survive more than a day or two without an urgent operation to increase the diameter of her windpipe.

There are only a handful of these operations, called "sliding tracheoplasties," performed off cardiopulmonary bypass each year, and the stakes are very high. The tissue is obviously small and quite delicate, so you have to be precise. I never saw or participated in a sliding tracheoplasty on a child during my training at Mayo, but I had done trachea surgery on adults. In short: It was going to be a major risk.

I made a few phone calls to senior mentors of mine. One told me that I was being too bold and too risky too soon in my career and advised me not to do the operation, but rather to send it to an older surgeon or center that had done a few of these. This was good advice, but the child was too ill and would not survive another transfer. So I decided to perform the operation the next morning.

I knew Anna's operation would be dangerous, and thus we were going to be under a lot of pressure. The day before surgery, while I was preparing to perform the operation, I dug out old intraoperative pictures of past operations of that kind. Infants are incredibly small lying on the operating-room table, so it helped me to view intraoperative pictures that I had taken of previous infant operations I had performed in order to accurately envision the operative field that I would see the next day. They allowed me to see myself and my hands in the arena interacting with this tiny infant. I visualized the operating room, the child on the operating-room bed, and then played the entire operation over in my mind again and again the night before the actual operation—along with many prayers and much tossing and turning.

The good Lord was with me and my team that day. The lights shone on us favorably. Anna did great, and was home in four days, without the need of a breathing machine. I got a Christmas card every year from her parents for several years, and then one day I got one from Anna herself. She is soon to enter college and is playing Division One sports. Apparently she can outrun most of her opponents.

You have to perform your best when the spotlight is brightest. An athlete, businessperson, or performer must recognize critical moments in their professional lives, as well as in their personal lives. Some moments are obvious: closing a big business deal, playing in the Super Bowl, deciding who you will marry. But some are not so obvious. A super performer has to recognize these moments and their critical significance and then excel at those times. There are some times when failure has much greater consequences than other times, and it's important to identify those times early in order to prepare for them adequately—just as Robby did on the pitcher's mound and as I did with my long night of study before operating on Anna.

There are certain times in life and certain critical moments in sporting events when you have to be bold and take a risk in order to win. Too many consider the reward without first fully considering the risk. This consideration also has to include an analysis of the timing of a risk, not just the question of your skill: Sometimes the timing is not best for your career. For example, if your company is currently losing money and another risky adventure may have a high upside but may also lead to bankruptcy, this is not the time to take the risk. There are times to be risk averse, and if it is a career decision, you have time to carefully consider the pluses and minuses and can apply objective decision making.

However, if it is an operation or a coaching decision, it can seem like you have only a few seconds to decide. In this case, if you decide to take the risk, you have to be right. There are some times you just cannot be wrong. That was the case with me and Anna, the two-day-old baby. In such situations, once you're sure the risk is acceptable, all boldness is warranted. Trust your instinct, be bold, and live with the consequences.

CHAPTER 3

Lifetime Commitment
to Super Performing

Living in the Moment

. . .

Sweeping the Dirt off the Rubber

Super Performing by
Staying in the Moment

One day during my cardiothoracic fellowship, as I was washing my hands at the scrub sink before starting the second coronary-artery bypass operation of the day, the attending surgeon told me that the patient we had just operated on one hour ago had died. He had an arrhythmia and coded, and they could not get him back. We were both devastated. But our next patient was already prepped and draped and in the next operating room, ready for his operation. One moment we were dejected and devastated, and the next we were sawing a patient's sternum.

As we started this new operation, I thought over and over again about whether we had done something wrong in the first operation. But we didn't do anything wrong. Every stitch was perfect, and the operation technically could not have gone better. I had just spoken to the patient's family and told them he was fine. It was amazing to me that a man we just operated on an hour earlier was now dead and that we had to go on immediately to the next operation. It seemed almost uncaring, but we had no choice. We had to go perform despite what had just happened and deliver another high performance—a perfect operation. And we did.

We accomplished this by renewing our intense attention to detail and by living in the moment. I have tried to teach many athletes and surgeons how to live in the moment and how to forget any mistakes or failures that may have just occurred. We cannot change them. They are over and done with. Right now, we need successful performance.

Whenever someone tells me how hard it can be to do this, I often put their performance into perspective by telling that story about back-to-back surgeries: It was the middle of a Little League baseball game. We had been ahead 8–3 going into the last inning, but we had just made three errors on three consecutive plays. The bases were loaded and there were two outs. The team was becoming demoralized.

"Live in the moment!" I yelled as I walked onto the baseball field, calling all of the infielders over to the mound. When they had gathered, I told them about the patient who had died while my surgical team and I had another one on the operating-room table, ready to go. The infield umpire, who had been listening, got closer and closer as I told the story. He was amazed that I was saying this now, to a bunch of ten-year-old kids.

After I finished telling the story, my first baseman, a large, lovable, six-foot-one boy, asked me, "Coach, what the heck is a coronary artery?" With that, we all laughed and walked off the mound.

Somehow the story relaxed them and helped them live in the moment. Their last batter hit a sharp ground ball to my first baseman, who made a nice play, and we won 8–7.

Although it is easy to say "Live in the moment and forget immediate past failures," it is difficult to do. We are all just human. Previous events affect our mood and our ability to further perform.

However, being able to separate those past events from our decision-making process and retaining emotional control is critical for a super performer. A super performer understands that that error is an isolated event—in other words, it's over. It is completely disconnected from the subsequent event that they are about to perform. We have to commit to preventing the feelings linked to that mistake in the past from affecting our future acts. We have to move onward. This mind-set allows a super performer to recheck, refocus, and deliver a super performance immediately.

It is interesting to watch teams—not just individuals, but different teammates—commit one unforced error or error in judgment and then compound it with another one very soon afterward. It is very common in baseball, especially Little League baseball. Why? Why does one ground ball through the shortstop's legs lead to the next ground ball going through the third baseman's legs? Or, during a rundown, you may see three consecutive throwing errors. Often a coach may yell, "It's contagious out there!" And perhaps the mind-set is contagious, which explains why one error seems to lead to the others. It is like a virus that spreads from one teammate to another.

But a professional does not allow one mistake to snowball into other mistakes. This only happens from emotional insecurity. It occurs if you allow the emotional ebbs and flows of the moment to affect your mind-set. A super performer recognizes this and prevents the downward trend. A relief pitcher in baseball is said to have a short memory, since he can blow a save one night and the very next night be back on the mound again pitching in a tight game, trying to get the same save. The mind-set of a surgeon should be the same as that of a relief pitcher. The only difference is that the pitcher is performing to save a baseball game whereas surgeons are often performing to save a life.

Any performer should have a prearranged reset point in their mind to deal with adversity. In the operating room, in the days before robotic surgery, I used to immerse my sterile gloved hands in a bowl of sterile warm water. I loved the feeling of the soothing warm water, and it helped me to relax, stay warm, and operate better. This is a specific example of one technique, but you should always have a similar prearranged routine that helps you reset your focus, concentration, and confidence if things are not going well during an event. If you are delivering a lecture and use the wrong word or make a mistake, you should have a preset method to regain your confidence. I taught one speaker to just say "Check that—I meant to say," fix the error, and move on immediately to the next slide.

All three of my boys are pitchers. I taught them at ages seven and eight to literally and figuratively sweep away the past negative events and live in the moment by taking their cleats and sweeping the dirt off of the rubber on the mound. It is another specific technique that does not bring too much attention to the performer, but that provides a mechanical method to reset their mind and disconnect from the previous negative events.

Another method is to use a spot on the field to remind yourself to refocus and reset mentally, ideally a spot that is a fixed, inanimate object that is visible from all parts of the field or the arena of play. In baseball, I used home plate when I was hitting and second base when I played shortstop. In the operating room, I used the blue sterile towels draped around the patient. No matter what negative event had just transpired, these fixed objects served a purpose: They allowed me to reset, refocus, start anew, and clear my mind of the negative events that had just happened a moment ago. Decide on one that works best for you and that can be easily, inconspicuously employed during the game or event so that your process is invisible to those around you.

The "No Lose" Scenario

One day on my Christmas vacation during my time at Mayo, I came home and my dad had an emergency consult. Since I had a New Jersey license, I went in and operated with him, which was both fun and a great honor. He was a great technical surgeon. The next day my brother, my dad, and I all went ice skating on a nearby pond and played hockey. Although he was seventy years old then, he was still in good shape.

A day later, I was back at work at Mayo, operating, when my mom called to tell me that my dad had had a heart attack. I was shocked: How could that be? He seemed so normal, so incredibly healthy just a day ago, so invulnerable. He was at the top of his game just yesterday on the ice, on the pond, and in the operating room.

But it was my job to ensure he got the proper care. It was my responsibility to get him through this ordeal.

I flew my parents out to Mayo the next day. My dad got a heart catheterization and then underwent open-heart surgery, a triple-bypass operation. I was a fellow then, and I had a large number of commitments. Some suggested that I cancel all of my commitments, but I wondered how I could honor them and still be there for my mom and dad.

I believed that I had a job to do. I had commitments to my attending surgeons, to my patients, and to the other residents and fellows in the program. The idea of taking time off from work for my father's triple bypass did not even occur to me. It never even entered my mind.

If you really care, you can fulfill all of your commitments both to work and to family. It just comes down to how hard you want to do them all and how willing you are to look for a workable scenario to get both done. I call it the "no lose" scenario. I wanted to be there for my mom and dad, but I also had to operate on two other patients who needed open-heart operations that day.

The next day, I operated in one operating room and did a coronary-artery-bypass graft on an elderly man from Minnesota, while my dad had his coronary-artery-bypass graft in the operating room next door. My plan was to be with him preoperatively and then to peek in to see how he was doing in his operating room between my own operations, as well as to go out intermittently to the waiting room in order to give my mom updates. This not only let me keep my work commitments, but was easier for me than it would have been to sit in the waiting room, knowing nothing and doing nothing. This plan worked well, and my dad and the other two patients we operated on that day all did well—at least, for the moment.

This wasn't the only time in my life that work and family commitments seemed to be in conflict. Another time, in 1992, I was a general surgical resident at the Mayo Clinic, and we had booked a very rare operation for Tuesday: an aorta-to-bilateral-carotid bypass graft, which essentially involves connecting the aorta to the two main carotid arteries in the neck.

Because of its rarity, I had been looking forward to this operation for a few days. But I was also looking forward to another important event: the birth of our first son, Robby. Lorraine was one day past her due date, and I did not want to let my attending surgeon down by missing the operation. So we gently convinced Lorraine's obstetrician to admit her in order to induce labor as soon as I got off of work that Monday afternoon.

It went great, Lorraine looked like a model, and Robby was born at 6:07 a.m., Tuesday morning, July 14, 1992. People often say that the birth of a child is one of the greatest days in your life, and it was for us. We were enthralled to be parents. But I was supposed to be in the operating room at 6:45 a.m. to get our patient ready for this rare operation. Today, male physicians take a two- to three-week paternity leave when they have a child. Back then, I felt guilty taking a fifteen-minute one. I told Lorraine that I had to run to be on time to the operating room, and she smiled in that way that only she could, and she said she understood and loved me.

We all have commitments in life. We all should articulate

and even write down our promises to our family members and to our coworkers. In addition, there are unspoken promises to them as well as to others in our lives. Too often, the commitments to the people at work take a backseat to those to the people at home. Yet the two events are rarely mutually exclusive, though too many people assume they are. You can be there for your kids' birthday parties, graduations, and Little League games and still get all your work done at your job with high quality if you have properly planned. Super performers realize this early because they are prepared, and then they strategize to find a way to get both done.

You can honor all of your commitments, both professional and personal, by planning your schedule weeks in advance. Communicate to your friends and family about what you have to do. Tell your partners and work colleagues about an upcoming important date or event so that they know you will not be there. Likewise, tell your children and spouse about important dates and events at work that you cannot miss. Let them know that you have a commitment to your work and your team members at work, and make sure they understand why you cannot be with them on time or at a specific event. If you need to make up time because you may have to leave work early or miss a day, then start making up the work you're going to miss long before the event occurs.

For unexpected events like family illness or true crises (of which there are very few), planning is not possible. However, you can plan your reaction to a crisis. Our current culture makes it too easy for people to completely drop all of their work commitments in order to tend to "family disasters" or "misfortunes." This too often unfairly burdens work colleagues who are apt to respond the same way when their own "family crisis" occurs.

The definition of "family crisis" has been twisted and abused by too many. Our culture is one that values understanding, concern, and compassion for most any type of health issue involving family members. This is desirable, and we should maintain this type of policy and genuine concern for the people we work with and for. However, I know several people who literally seem to go to a family or "close friend's" funeral every other week for months. Clearly this is not what our society had in mind when we first enacted these policies.

Before you say you just cannot honor a professional or personal commitment, spend a little time trying to figure out an ingenious solution to do both. You may not find yourself looking through an operating-room window with a surgical mask on, watching your father's sternum being sawed apart as he undergoes an open-heart operation as you scrub your own hands to perform an operation of your own, but you may find yourself in unique situations. And at the end of the day, you will be proud of yourself and happy because you found a way to make everyone happy and fulfill your commitments to everyone.

Super Performers Never Take a Vacation from Super Performing

There's significant data to support the idea that vacations offer an important time to allow the mind and body to relax and unwind. However, gorging yourself with fatty food for seven days straight, sleeping late, not exercising, and abusing alcohol is not the recipe that a super performer applies on his or her vacation. The idea is to find a new way to challenge the mind and body.

So plan events on your vacation that are both mentally and physically challenging—especially events that might incorporate the entire family. It is important to relax and unwind, but most of us truly only need a few days. Use your vacation time to explore new challenges. Lorraine and I only took several days of vacation a year. We would either go on a cruise and go scuba diving, or climb trees, or visit my parents' home in Florida. In Florida, we would go to a nearby baseball park most every day and practice skills with the kids, as well as to the beach to play sports in the sand.

We would also work out as a family almost every day. We would try all different kinds of workouts as a family, such as P90X, T25, Insanity, and Asylum. This can be fun if you, as the parent, make it fun. Create a culture in your family and at work in which competing, getting smarter, and getting in great physical shape is a source of fun rather than dread.

Corporate America should embrace this concept of mixing fun with work as well. The head of a corporation or the leader of a team should have his team members get together at least once a year outside of work at retreats, which can and should involve sports and other structured activities. This allows employees to get away from the daily grind of the repeated rigors of work, but also to compete and get better together as they unwind and fire neurons in new patterns. (Learning a new problem set is always a good thing for the mind.) Leadership workshops can lead to team building and better relationships between employees. This "vacation" time provides rest and recharging of the battery, and the nighttime can be used to further get to know one another over food and wine and form important relationships that improve work productivity. You should meet and talk with one another's spouses and significant family members. This leads to better appreciation of one another at the workplace and reminds us that they are not just colleagues with whom you may be upset from time to time—they're also somebody's mom or spouse. By engaging with these others, we can appreciate one another a little better and understand how interdependent we all are on one another.

Finally, you can find ways to incorporate your work life more directly into your vacation by finding ways to practice your trade while vacationing. Most people on vacation do not perform the same job they do at work—in particular, most surgeons on vacation do not operate, and especially not with their fathers, as I did. However, many go on mission trips to operate on indigent patients across the world. This may or may not be right for you, but it's worth considering finding ways to go on vacation without losing your connection to your skill set.

For example, during the summer when the kids and we were practicing baseball intensely day after day, I decided my three boys needed to take a few days off. They did not seem to be having fun one afternoon. So I rented out an ice rink near my home. We ice skated and played football and baseball on ice. We even had a baseball game on ice. It brought the fun back to the game while the kids, without knowing it, were working on their balance and core strength while playing baseball on skates.

A Major Injury Is Only One Play Away

Although my father's open-heart operation had initially gone well, eight hours after the close, there was still blood in his chest tubes and he was still on the ventilator long after he should have been off. He was in trouble, and it looked like he might have to go back to the operating room. I remember seeing him on the ventilator: He had never looked so fragile to me, so vulnerable. How could this larger-than-life figure—a man whom I had just ice skated with and operated with a few days ago—be reduced to this pale, weak, elderly man barely clinging to life on a respirator?

My mind flashed back to when I was a boy and we were cutting trees in our backyard woods. My dad's chain saw came to a sudden halt, and suddenly blood was pouring out of his right hand and he was holding pressure on his index finger to minimize the bleeding. I remember packing the distal finger in snow, thinking silently what I knew my dad was also thinking: This could be a career-ending injury for a surgeon.

"I'll be fine," he said as we walked into the house.

We drove to the emergency room and within an hour he was in the operating room. The surgeon finally came out and told the rest of us that my dad's finger would be fine and that he should be able to resume operating without any problems.

This injury could have cost my father his career. It could have been the last time he ever operated. We all take so much of our lives for granted, especially our health. Everyone is subject to injury, and an injury can occur in an instant. But professional athletes and surgeons are especially attuned to this risk because we rely so much on our physical skills to perform and earn a living.

Injury is always right around the corner, especially when playing contact sports. I realized that as I was skating fast down the far wing in a 3–3 hockey game just a few years ago. I was playing in a men's hockey league tournament. I was in for a breakaway, but the defensemen tripped me from behind. I lost control and collided with the lead pipes of the hockey goal. But as much as it hurt, it was the finals of a hockey tournament, so I, like most every other hockey player I know, refused to come out.

That night I had severe pain, and I got a chest X-ray (CXR) that showed I had broken two ribs. The next morning, I had several long operations, including a lobectomy for lung cancer on a well-known politician. With ACE bandages and a topical lidocaine patch, I was able to operate fine.

We cannot live in a protective bubble. Why would a surgeon own a chain saw or play hockey? I enjoy it. It is a part of who and what I am. Once you construct a bubble around your life you are no longer living it, but just going through the motions.

But still, life is fragile. One minute you are perfectly healthy, the next you may be seriously injured. Emergency rooms serve as a morbid and stark reminder to our younger generation that they are not invincible. We all take our health for granted—you have too, to some extent. And it's just not practical to thank God every minute of every day for being healthy. But maybe we should thank Him once a day at least.

My dad and I enjoyed working in the yard. We liked cutting down old trees and chopping them into firewood. But I never dreamed that that day with the chainsaw would be the last time we did this. Because of that event, he never operated a chain saw again. I never dreamed, the morning at the age of fifty when I sat in the hockey locker room and tightened my skate, that this day would be my last competitive hockey tournament game—I had been playing hockey once a week for almost forty-six years—but it probably was. The risk to my patients was too high. I still miss being surrounded by my teammates and their comradely repartee and banter in the locker room.

Those thoughts—that the time you're currently doing an activity you enjoy will be the last time you perform that activity—never occurred to me, just as it never occurs to most people until they suffer an injury that takes it all away in an instant. I just assumed that another day was coming. Another day filled with the same healthy friends and family members was always just twenty-four hours away, I thought. But I was wrong. It is not.

So appreciate days you have that are filled with loved ones and with activities you have taken for granted.

Special moments do not occur just with family, but at work as well. Some of us spend more time with our work colleagues than we do our family members. A super performer understands the special events at work and makes the effort to take time out to make them memorable. In addition, he or she understands that even the routine day—performing when the lights are bright, as we do in the operating room—is special. A super performer learns to appreciate all of these moments and shows others how to view them as special as well.

When special moments with family are approaching, realize how special they are, and realize that they may not always be there. It may not be just another Thanksgiving dinner with your family and friends. So decide before you go to control your anger from the typical family comments that may usually set you off. Rise above the petty arguments and savor the special moments. Your family moments are finite, so cherish them all. Bring a camera to keep memories of the event. (We should take more pictures in our lives. Fortunately, that is happening now with cell phones. Videos are great as well.)

Even when it's not a special occasion, take a few minutes every now and then to look around the table at your home and at work. Thank the people you work with for being part of your life and for everything they do for you. Thank your family for honoring the promises they have made and kept, and for all they do. They may think that you are crazy—or even ask if you are dying or going somewhere—but do it anyway.

Make every event in your life as special as you can. Even something like cutting trees in the woods with your father may be a more important and memorable event then you think.

The Fragility of Life

When you are feeling wonderful, life is going great, and you rise out of bed invigorated without any physical afflictions, take a second to appreciate it. Stay humble during these times, because—as we've seen—an injury may be closer than you think. Be kind to others in your family and at work on your team. You may need your teammates around you when you're hurting more than you ever thought, so be humble and treat them well when you are healthy and productive.

But it's not enough just to be appreciative of your health: You also have to work actively on staying healthy. A critical aspect of a super performer's life is physical fitness. You cannot perform well in most things if you are not physically fit. What's more, there's scientific data to support the idea that physical fitness helps mental fitness.

Many companies are starting to understand this concept. Some have incentivized their employees to work out during their lunch break, lose weight, stop smoking, and lower their blood pressure by reducing individual health-care premiums for those employees who improve their health. This strategy leads to better alignment of the values of the employees and the company, making both leaner and more productive. Most companies have a strict policy on moral ethics and behavior, but not one on health behavior—why? We should have a no-tolerance policy for "lack of wellness" in the work place, just as we do not tolerate harassment or discrimination.

Health is one of the most valuable commodities we have and one of the most abused. Most of us are born with it, but few of us are fully invested in maintaining or improving it. To fully appreciate your health takes maturity and time; children can rarely do it. (Events that take it away serve as a stark reminder, but that is a tough way to learn.)

It takes a daily and total commitment to maintain health. No matter how busy we get with work and family commitments, we have to exercise at least three (or even better, five) times a week to maintain a basic level of fitness. We need about twenty to thirty minutes of exercise with each workout—with a heart rate that is at least 50 percent above your baseline—in order to fully reap the benefits of cardiovascular exercise. Muscle building is a supplemental exercise that we need to do as well, especially as we get older, and is usually independent of a cardiovascular workout. Finally, stretching, core strength, and flexibility become more and more important as we age. These are a critical aspect of a super performer's life.

Most injuries are not a reason to avoid exercise. I hear every day from obese patients in my clinic that they cannot exercise because their knees hurt or their backs hurt. I sympathize, but obesity only makes those problems worse. Back and knee pain are not reasons not to exercise. They're just reasons to modify the type of workout you do. Swim or stretch, but get active in one form or another. Whatever your situation, working out should be thought of like brushing your teeth—it is a necessary part of every day.

Since we all have to do it, I decided long ago to make working out part of our family time as well. Lorraine and I started working out with our kids when they were just four and five years old, and I still do it today. If you do this as well, you'll be teaching your children a great lifelong lesson. You are inculcating healthy habits and leading by example. In addition, by working out together as a family, you are spending quality time together and challenging one another to get better—as well as getting your own workout in.

With One Swing of the Bat

One night when I got home, my three kids were swimming in my pool with the next-door-neighbor boys. At the time, my kids were two, five, and eight years old, and the other boys were about nine and ten. I had performed eleven operations that day, and I was tired.

Matthew, my youngest, was still not an independent, safe swimmer at that time, but he was close. Robby came out of the pool and wanted a towel, and I went into the house to get it. Lorraine and another couple were sitting at the poolside watching the five boys. When I came back out to the pool, I started to sit down with Lorraine and the couple next door. I asked them where Matthew was, as I did not see him clinging to the side of the pool in the shallow end like he was when I left.

Then I saw him. It is an image that is forever ingrained in my mind's eye.

Matthew's limp body was lying on the bottom of our deep end, his blue diaper bathing suit–clad body lying in a fetal position. He was motionless, lying calmly under ten feet of crystal-clear water, looking as if he were sound asleep on the bottom of our pool.

Despite having my shirt, tie, and shoes on, I jumped in and pulled him out. His limp arms and legs dangled as I carried him out of the water: This is the image Lorraine always remembered. He had no pulse. So I started cardiopulmonary resuscitation (CPR). Chest compression, chest compression, breathe, breathe. His lips were cold and purple, and his skin was ashen. I carried on: chest compression, chest compression, breathe, breathe. Nothing, no response.

I asked Lorraine to call 911 and the UAB's children's emergency room and to request a helicopter. She yelled that it was on the way, and then she kneeled down next to us and prayed. I told her that prayers were good, but right now, I needed her help with Matthew. The neighbors took all four young boys away to their house to prevent further lifelong visual and mental scars. Lorraine turned on the lights on the basketball court so that the helicopter could see where to land. I kept doing CPR: chest compression, chest compression, breathe, breathe. His lips were still blue, and there was no response.

Then a strange thought entered my mind. To this day, I am ashamed and embarrassed to relate it, but it happened. I considered stopping and letting Matthew go. I am not sure why. It is disgraceful that this thought would even enter a father's mind, especially one who was a surgeon and who had performed CPR on strangers' hearts for much longer periods of time. I had performed CPR for over two hours on Dylan, the young boy at Mayo. Why would I consider stopping on my own son after just two or three minutes? What was wrong with me? Perhaps I feared he would live but suffer an anoxic brain injury. He was so smart and such a good athlete at two, and he had so much promise. Maybe, knowing that, I was too selfish to want to have to care for an invalid.

But the thought lasted only for an instant. I quickly

dismissed it and went back to work, not missing a beat of the CPR—back to chest compressions and breathing. And I was glad I had dismissed it, because twenty seconds later Lorraine, kneeling beside me, yelled, "I feel a radial pulse; it's getting stronger!"

I checked his carotid. There was a definite pulse, though weak. After ten seconds, it had become stronger. Matthew was back; he was alive.

I stopped the CPR and quickly rolled him over, because I knew he was going to vomit next. He did. My wife had prepared risotto, one of our favorite meals, earlier that day for dinner. Now it was sitting in a heap at my poolside, only partially digested. But Matthew was getting better quickly, and he was breathing well. I rolled him onto his back again. Lorraine ran into the house and got my stethoscope. His heart and lungs sounded great.

By now there were two police cars and an ambulance in my driveway, their blue and red flashing signals lighting up the trees surrounding my lower driveway. (The helicopter was called off.) The entire scene was surreal. I scooped Matthew up in my arms and carried him to the ambulance truck. This time his arms clung to me tightly.

As soon as we hit the ER doors, I started barking orders: "I want a stat CXR and an IV started, right now!" I yelled. The pediatric ER doctor told me to relax, that Matthew would be fine, and that Lorraine and I should get counseling. I am embarrassed to say it, but I went ballistic. I told her to do her job, to get in there and take care of my son and stop the psychoanalytical mumbo jumbo. Additionally, I told her I wanted her to describe, in detail, her plan to prevent hyponatremia and re-expansion pulmonary edema, and to check Matthew's sodium levels immediately. I want to apologize to her now for my actions that night. I am sorry.

But in one hour, Matthew was jumping around that ER as if nothing had happened. Lorraine and I spent the next hour quizzing him on old family pictures, about characters in his books, and about his ABCs. Lorraine spent the whole night in the hospital at his side. She never went to sleep that entire night, never took her eyes off his oxygen saturation. He did fine.

That night, while Lorraine watched Matthew, my other two sons and I talked for a long time about what had happened. I told my sons that I had let Matthew down. I had not fulfilled my responsibility as a parent, and we had failed him as a family. We were not there for him. We did not watch him closely enough. We talked about how fragile life can be. Although they were only eight and five years old, they understood it as well as they could at their level. I put them to bed, but first I told them that they were still going to their sports practices tomorrow because they had responsibilities to meet and they had summer-school worksheets to do. I told them that I was going to operate the next day as well because I had responsibilities to my patients and their families and a job to do. Finally, I told them that Matthew would be fine.

I then walked out to the pool. The pool lights seemed to flicker differently under the water's ripples. I kneeled down by the risotto—now covered with ants—and I prayed. I thanked God for his grace and for taking care of Matthew and for giving me my son back. I thanked him for his guidance and for our positive and lucky outcome. I told him that I was sorry I was not there for my son, and that it would not happen again.

It was June 12, 2000. I now call June 12 Matthew Cole Day. It was both the worst and best day of my life.

The next morning in the operating room, several of my partners told me I should not have been operating, but I had a job to do and a commitment to my patients to fulfill. The operations all went well, and I came home early the next day to spend time with Matthew, who was already back home. As I drove up our quiet street around four p.m., I could see him running in the backyard, kicking the soccer ball with Lorraine running after him. It was a glorious sunny day. I will never forget that image. It was one of the happiest moments in my life. I stopped in the middle of the road and I smiled and thanked God again. I quickly ran onto the lawn and tackled him. We wrestled, and he giggled, and as he ran back down the lawn, chasing the soccer ball, Lorraine and I grasped each other's hand and held them tight behind and smiled at one another and said how much we loved each other.

I'll never forget the smell of the chlorine on my shirt from that day. I still have that shirt in my closet to this day, and I saved Matthew's swimsuit in my car for three years.

It is normal to get nervous before big events or during a disaster. I may have seemed very calm to my family and our neighbors during this horrible ordeal, but inside I was not calm. I was working hard and thinking of everything I could possibly do to get Matthew through it. But I learned, once again, how quickly life can change. How in an instant life can be dramatically and permanently changed.

It's indisputable, however, that my training had helped to prepare me for this critical moment. In moments like these, you have to be able to control your emotions and perform under pressure. It's just like a duck: He appears to be gliding along the surface of a pond, but underneath, his legs and feet are frantically working to keep himself afloat.

Controlling your nerves—or at least appearing to control them on the surface, appearing to glide along the surface— is a direct product of the amount of preparation you do. The more you prepare, the less likely you are to be nervous. If you are to give an important presentation, there is nothing like going to the lectern you will be standing in front of and practicing without stopping. Force yourself to perform as expertly as if it were game day.

When leading others in practice, intentionally add pressure to the situation. For example, during basketball practices I coached, each player had to make a free throw consecutively. I wanted all twelve players to make it, and the pressure mounted on the next shooter: If he missed, we had to start all over back at zero. Additionally, I always had the worst player go last. No one could go home until we did it as a team. This led to the team rooting for one another and for the best players to help the worst players to get better. I did the same in infield practice with my baseball team. We had to record nine consecutive outs, and I hit ground balls or fly balls to every player—and again, usually to the worst player last. If he made an error, we had to start all over as a team. This makes the teammates pull for one another and feel the pressure of everyone relying on them. If they made an error, it hurt the team, not just them. They understood that they were only as strong as their weakest link, and thus it behooved each player to make one another better. Super performers understand the importance of making their teammates better as well as themselves.

Anxiety management—which is discussed in detail later in this book—is an important part of performance under pressure. By using techniques such as visualization and breathing, we can slow down our minds during critical moments. If you invoke your brain more during anxiety-provoking physical events (a big game or a dangerous operation) and think about the next step you have to do, your mind will allow your body to perform the current step on autopilot, just as you have done in practice a thousand times. When you learn how to mentally anticipate just a few moments ahead, your physical skills become very relaxed. Your own muscle memory takes over the current step you are performing and allows your mind to get out of your body's way. Stay one step ahead by thinking of every possible permutation that can happen.

Apparently some people were impressed that I could perform CPR so calmly on my own son. Yet in between breaths, I thought of moving the sports equipment off of the lawn so that the helicopter had a spot to land, turning the lights on so that they could see our house, getting a drowning expert to the hospital, and so on. Because I was thinking about those next steps, in essence, I was doing CPR on autopilot. I was not even thinking about it or how to do it, and thus I looked very relaxed doing it. Instead, I was constantly thinking about the next thing we had to do to achieve the outcome I desired: my son alive and well. (And as you've read, thanks to some prayers and the good Lord, we got the outcome we wanted.)

Learn a New Pitch Every Season

When I first saw robotic surgery, I honestly believed it was just an expensive gimmick. I thought it was too expensive and could not improve my patients' outcomes. And why did I need to learn it? We already had one of the busiest and most highly regarded thoracic surgical programs in the world. We had patients and visitors coming from all over the world to have surgery by us or to watch us operate as a team. We also had some of the best results and most profitable programs in the world.

Against all of that, the robot was an entirely new way to do surgery. I would have to start all over to learn it. It was a paradigm shift. It was going to slow me down, put me and my team back on the learning curve, reduce my efficiency—and maybe even possibly hurt some patient inadvertently as we learned the technology. Yet after realizing what the technology was capable of, I knew that the lack of adoption in thoracic surgery was due to political and monetary issues—not patient outcomes. I also knew that this was the best way I was going to deliver better care for my patients in the future.

It was very tough sledding at first. However, after two years, we have developed the world's busiest robotic thoracic program and have reduced our blood loss, our pain scores, and our mortality from 1.4 percent to 0.2 percent. The improvements aren't limited to the use of robots: I have also trained residents to hold instruments in different ways so they can perform more consistently and reliably when under pressure from severe bleeding.

This process is no different for athletes who are already successful but who want to get better. For example, athletes are commonly trying new shots, new moves, or even new equipment. Tiger Woods had a very successful year a few years ago, yet he changed his swing to try to make it more reproducible when under pressure. A Cy Young–level pitcher knows he needs to get even better for next year, and thus he should learn a new pitch every year.

When an athlete has this mind-set and accomplishes this, the results can be spectacular. My son Robby illustrated this nicely on a cold day in March in New York City. Robby was a sophomore at Yale pitching against the Columbia Lions. He was pitching a complete game but losing. He had a great changeup, and he was using it frequently. It had been his most effective pitch of the day, but it was late in the game, he was already on his third time through their lineup, and his best pitch was no longer a great surprise. So he decided to introduce his new changeup, one that he had never thrown in a game before but that we had worked on over the summer. The next three batters went down swinging because they had never seen this pitch before. During those summer months, many people had asked us: Why were we tinkering with his best pitch? Watch the videotape of that game and the answer becomes clear: to get better.

New ways to train or exercise apply to all of us, especially if it concerns our general health. New ideas should always be considered and never dismissed. The first time I saw a P90X infomercial on television, I knew this extreme workout program would be a great mental and physical challenge for my family and me. I also knew that it would be a new opportunity for us to learn a lot about commitment, accountability, and perseverance.

The month before we started P90X, I had been running a one-mile race with my three boys every day. I made them sign a contract that we would do it daily for two months. They did not know how much I loathed that run after a long day at work. I remember getting viscerally sick on my car ride home just thinking about it. But I did it because my kids held me accountable. We used the same technique to commit to P90X. Over the next few years we as a family did P90X, P90X Plus, and P90X2 programs, and we all signed a contract that we would finish each one. And we did.

What I learned from these exercise programs (P90X, P90X2, Insanity, Asylum, and T25) is that few people really do their maximum. They are too quick to quit and too quick to stop. Only the best super performers push themselves to get better.

Thus, any new training programs that offer a new way or perspective or approach to accomplishing a task should be evaluated, and many should be adopted. The fallout or by-product of trying new techniques may take you in a direction you could never have expected. Many successful businesses have been born from the unexpected by-product of trying a new idea or a concept that failed, but that led them in another direction. If you never try, you'll never open those doors.

So keep an open mind, carefully read and study in your area of expertise, and talk constantly to other leaders in your field or discipline. As a super performer, you can never be satisfied with your status, even if you are at the top of your field. Strengthen your strengths, not just your weaknesses. We must all be willing to evolve.

The Rewards of Teaching

When we are young, we are focused on ourselves and how to make ourselves better. But at the end of the day, we all start to realize that none of life is entirely about ourselves—it is all about making those around us better. A true super performer does this instinctively. Once you have made yourself and your own individual skills as good as you can, it then becomes incumbent on you to make your teammates as good as they can be as well.

Internal competition, of course, has a place. In terms of team building, internal competition between high-quality people is the best way to make a team strong—even a surgical team. I have hired the best thoracic surgeons in the world. Some professors or divisional chairs are afraid that if their junior faculty is too good, they will eventually take their practice away or retire them. The reality is that yes, this will—and should—eventually happen. By hiring people who provide you with strong internal competition, you create a strong legacy for the program as a whole. A good leader will hire the best people around him. This will make him better as well. Great internal competition is critical for external success.

But although we are all competitive—and no one is more competitive than I—it's important to remember that surgery is not ultimately a competition, but a matter of life and death. A patient's life is on the line, and they're counting on our performance, not on our competitiveness with one another. The more we can help our surgical colleagues improve, the better care all of our patients get. We should strive to create the same atmosphere that surrounds a baby learning to walk for the first time—no one belittles the infant when he loses his balance and falls.

We have many hospitals that border UAB, and I have had many of their thoracic surgeons come to our operating room to learn our techniques. I am honored to teach them and to have them take time out of their practice to observe our team. The better they get, the better we have to get. A rising tide does indeed lift all boats and most importantly, it provides better care to more patients.

This is why teaching, for me, has become so rewarding. I have always enjoyed teaching medical students, residents, and fellows. I have used the Socratic method rather than simple lecturing when teaching. If a student answers incorrectly, they will never forget the right answer, whereas if you present the fact in a lecture format, it is more easily forgotten. Surgeons learn from their mistakes as well, and we all try to learn from one another's mistakes by discussing them at conferences.

My epiphany to help other attending surgeons operate and to serve as a coach to other surgeons started a few years ago and has blossomed in the past few years. I've begun to teach full-fledged surgeons who were long done with their training and many professors at major medical teaching centers all over the world. I have developed protocols for many parts of the operation, from how the patient goes into the operating room, to how they are anesthetized and how each and every aspect of an operation is done, down to the most minute detail. We have created a reliable and reproducible technique that the surgeon—like an athlete with a playbook—can fall back on and use to perform when under great pressure.

Two or three years ago, I helped a well-known surgeon at a major academic center do his first robotic operation. We had just finished the operation, and I was taking off my surgical gloves, something I had done a million times before, when the surgeon said: "Thanks for helping me, man, thanks for coming here and helping me and my team elevate our game. Thanks for taking the time to come out here and leave your busy practice."

Hearing that, I felt great, just as I had twenty-five years earlier when I was a surgical intern and performed my first operation. I remember calling Lorraine immediately from just outside the academic center's operating rooms and telling her how satisfied I was, professionally and personally. I told her how happy it made me feel to help someone—especially someone on this level, who was world famous—was actually thanking me.

"Then you should go ahead and do more of it," she said. It gave my life more purpose: a higher calling, a new calling.

We are all here to teach those around us, and fittingly, the word *doctor*, in Latin, means "teacher."

CHAPTER 4

Proper Preparedness

Responding to Adversity with Mental Agility

. . .

Practicing the Way We Play

Prepare for Disaster

"What is that funny-looking Satinsky clamp doing on your nurses' back table?" asked my visiting surgeon from Brazil. He was referring to a very long and slender clamp.

I told him that I rarely use it, but that one day about a year ago I was glad I had it on the field. I was doing what should have been a straightforward lobectomy in a young woman with lung cancer. However, when the vascular stapler was placed on the inferior pulmonary vein (a large vein that drains blood from the lung into the left side of the heart), it became literally stuck on the base of the heart.

We were in real trouble, and my options were few. I could just try to pull it off or try to pry the jaws of the stapler open, but this risked tearing a large hole in the base of the heart. This would cause massive bleeding and might also suck air into the left side of the patient's heart, which would lead to a stroke. But luckily—or preparedly—I had the Satinsky clamp ready for just such a disaster. I opened the pericardium, dissected out the vein off of the atrium, and then carefully slipped the Satinsky clamp just below the stapler. Then we cut the vein between the stapler and Satinsky. Now I could remove the stapler from the operative field and sew up the vein at the base of the heart without any problems.

In-depth, true preparation takes time and requires the super performer to carefully consider all the things that might go wrong. This is true in sports as well as in the operating room.

It was the biggest baseball game of Robby's life. He was ten years old, and he was the starting pitcher in the Alabama State Little League all-star final game. The game was televised on a local station. We had had a great season, but one of our only two losses was to the team we were playing in the finals. We had won the state championship the year before, and our expectation was to win it again. If we lost, the season would be considered a failure.

I found out later that one of TV announcers was commenting on how impressed he was that one of the coaches— that was me—was throwing ball after ball off the back brick wall behind the catcher, showing him and the pitchers the unusual bounces the ball could take at this particular ball park. He said that even though he had announced many college and even some professional baseball games, he had never seen a coach spend so much time preparing his battery (the catcher and pitchers) in quite this fashion. He even mentioned that I had walked off the distance between home plate and the brick wall three times.

The reason I made all these specific, detailed preparations was simple. During these baseball games played by ten-year-olds, it is common to get many passed balls and wild pitches. The boys are just not consistent enough at that age to prevent them. And although it is rare to get an out at home when there is a runner on third, I wanted to prepare my team the best I could. I gave them a grid system so Robby, the pitcher, could yell to the catcher where the ball was located when it landed behind him.

And that preparation paid off: During the game we had three wild pitches with men on third, and twice we got the catcher to throw the ball to Robby, who was covering home, and we tagged runners out at the plate. We won that game, and the state championship, 3–2.

True preparedness comes in many forms in sports, life, and surgery. Two weeks before the president of the United States came to Birmingham to lecture, I was paid a visit by several federal employees. They asked me, along with several other surgeons, to "be on call" in case the president was shot. This literally meant that I had to have one operating room empty for the entire time the president was in the Birmingham area. Not only did they pay a visit to me and to our operating rooms, but they also spoke to other surgeons in almost every conceivable specialty. They prepared for almost all types of injury that the president might suffer. They had detailed maps of the roads from his lecture to UAB Hospital, detailed maps of the hospital itself, our operating room, and all the back stairwells in our hospital. We saw Secret Service men on the rooftop the next day as well, getting prepared. Their preparation was impressive for a brief four-hour visit to Birmingham, Alabama. Thankfully their expertise was not needed, but this is thankfully true for most disasters.

We all know that when dealing with human systems, disasters and errors are never going to be completely preventable. Fortunately, disaster rarely occurs, but detailed and true preparation for disaster helps to prevent stress when it does. In addition, preparation can help to prevent some disasters because preparation forces one to ask how disasters might happen in the first place.

How can you prepare for an event that is unthinkable? By definition, you can't, or else it would be thinkable. However, you can try to prepare for all of the thinkable scenarios, and this may get you close to the unthinkable.

Most companies and hospitals have disaster-ready plans for major incidents—an earthquake, a flood, a plague—that bring many patients to the emergency room all at once. Disasters that happen on a smaller scale—such as in your operating room, at your business, or on the athletic field—have to first be considered before you can plan for them. Look around your workplace and ask yourself what five to ten terrible things could go wrong right now. Then start devising plans to prevent them and plans to deal with them if they occur.

To assist in this, you can ask others who have gone before you—in your current role or in a similar role—what some of the worst mistakes they've made have been. How did they deal with those mistakes, and what have they done since to avoid making them again? Additionally, what disasters did they plan for, and how? We do this at medical conferences all the time, and it is extremely informative. (It also takes great courage to present your worst mistakes.)

If you own a manufacturing business, you should carefully review the possible disastrous events that could happen at each stage of the process. Then take time to consider the possible branch points of these various scenarios and try to change your system to help avoid them. Each possible error should have a carefully devised plan that enables you to fix disasters when they occur, as well as to prevent disasters from happening in the first place. Even if you did not anticipate the actual event exactly, this process will make you and your team more likely to handle almost all of the unthinkable disasters as well as the thinkable.

Practice the Way You'll Play

Simulation is great, but only when it mimics the real deal. The statement "You play the way you practice" is true, but it is only half of the equation. The key is to practice under the conditions you are going to play. The better you can simulate playing conditions, the more effective the practice is, and the easier it will be to play the way you practice.

Performance under pressure is often the problem. Some people are fine in practice but underperform under the pressure of the actual event. Practice therefore has to find a way to simulate the pressure situation of a game. As I described in the previous chapter, we created pressure situations for our athletes during practice, and the same logic applies in other endeavors. For companies, you should have your employees who talk to clients or who make presentations practice in front of the entire office staff before sending them out to the customer. But this is not enough. In order to duplicate the pressure, you should let them know that after each salesperson presents, only one will be given a cash award. This creates pressure and healthy internal competition, which is critical for external success.

For coaches, there are many techniques you can use to create internal competition. Put your best kids against one another in practice so that the best compete against the best. In addition, I had my kids in Little League basketball literally taunt one another in a joking manner and make fun of each other as we were attempting free throws, just as would happen in a real game.

My batting cage is outside for a reason. I wanted the boys to practice hitting under the same conditions as in the game. An indoor batting facility eliminates the sun, heat, the wind, and all the other elements that a game presents. This is why I never put a roof over our batting cage, even though it meant we could not hit on days it rained. A few times I even set up large fans in front of them as they hit, piped in crowd noise, and tried to sprinkle some water onto their bats and their faces as they hit, to simulate hitting in the drizzle.

Efficient Practicing via Videotaping

The medical student was not quite sure what I was doing when I started filming him with my camcorder in the operating room. He did not know that I was going to use it to teach him, the general surgeon resident, and the cardiothoracic fellow. After we finished operating, we reviewed the videotape, and the fellow was amazed to see how he stood. "No wonder my knees and back are sore," he said.

Video does not lie, and it allows us to see ourselves in a different way. One of the best educational and teaching aspects of robotic surgery is that every operation we perform is videotaped. We had lots of frustration and challenges both mentally and physically in adapting to the new robotic surgical process. But the video allowed me to devise a new way to use all four robotic arms during an operation. We now teach this technique, and it is used all over the world. I had already been using videotape analysis to help my three boys run, hit, and throw better. Now I was using it to help younger surgeons operate better. We started to review the video after every operation, just as we did after every ball game.

One operation we perform for patients with esophageal cancer is called an esophagogastrectomy. A critical phase of this operation involves carefully placing about thirty small sutures that connect the esophagus to the new esophagus made out of the stomach. If these are not placed just perfectly, the patient can leak food and saliva into the chest. Some die from this complication. It is a long operation (five to six hours) and has a very high risk.

Recently we performed one of these operations on an eighty-two-year-old man. Although it went well technically in the operating room, the patient died about thirty-five days after the operation. He did not have a leak, but he developed pneumonia and never recovered. As a team, we carefully reviewed the entire operation and each of the thirty sutures we had placed in the anastomosis. We scrutinized the precise technical details of the entire operation. Then we went back to the operating room and practiced it again and again from beginning to end, making subtle changes. Even though there appeared to be nothing on the tape that we could have done differently, we tried to improve our process.

Too often after a loss, people are too quick to conclude,

"I tried my hardest, prepared my best, and there was nothing else I or we could have done differently." A super performer should always seek out new ways to practice and prepare better after a win, but especially after a loss.

Alec, my middle son, was having problems bunting down the first-base line. In order to fix this problem, we went to the batting cage in my backyard. It has a pitching machine and four high-definition slow-motion cameras, as well as a videotape-review area. We carefully examined his bunting technique in super slow motion. We found a technical flaw in his footwork that was accounting for his inability to bunt down the first-base line. The videotape review allowed us to quickly identify the problem and fix it. Video review affords instant feedback that quickly allows one to see oneself, diagnose a problem by reviewing a stance frame by frame with an expert, and finally practice better and more efficiently.

Obviously, there are some activities, such as athletic skills, that lend themselves more toward videotaping than others. However, almost any activity can be videotaped. I have videotaped a coach giving signs at third base to show him how he looks, an attending physician practicing a lecture, and a friend of mine in sales practicing his sales pitch.

Videotaping yourself can be difficult and embarrassing, but there are strategies to counteract this. If you have to give an important speech or presentation, you can videotape yourself in the privacy of your own home. If you are a CEO who leads a meeting of the board of directors, have someone videotape the next meeting and carefully watch it in privacy. Whatever method you use, it's clear that videotape analysis allows you to remove yourself from the moment, see yourself, and serve as your own coach. You will be amazed at how you look and sound on camera, and you'll learn something as well.

Above all, videotape helps to encourage efficient practice. Most understand the importance of practice, but too many spend a lot of time practicing inefficiently—or even worse, practicing the wrong moves. To be "the first guy at practice and the last one home" is a good mantra, but only if you are practicing the right things in the correct manner. Efficient practicing makes practice more fun, shorter, and more intensely productive, as well as reducing the time spent away from family.

The best way to practice efficiently is to invest more time in outlining the practice. Of course, it depends on what you are practicing for. For surgeons, until recently, all practice occurred on game day: in the operating room while operating on living patients under the tutelage of an attending experienced surgeon. However, now we have simulators and practice labs for all types of surgical techniques. We have carefully researched the best way to learn certain skills and then the best way to teach them.

In the first day of our robotic simulation lab, I spend time teaching the surgeon the best way to sit at the robotic console and the different ways to place their fingers in the hand controls. This establishes good habits. How you start an activity is often how you do it for a long time. Therefore, initial good habits are critical to help avoid developing bad habits. Then, videotape review allows the subject to more quickly correct mistakes.

Rehabilitation Starts the Day of Your Injury

I had just finished performing a long, difficult robotic lobectomy that took over four hours. I was still learning how to sit and operate for that long at the robotic console; I was used to standing for ten hours and operating, but not used to sitting. My back and neck were sore, and I knew I had to make some adjustments. Doing more P90X abdominal rippers was not the answer; I needed to fix this problem and fix it fast if I were to continue using this surgical tool.

So I carefully reviewed my ergonomics, examining the details of the chair as well as letting a medical student film me while I was operating robotically. I discovered that despite the multiple ergonomic adjustments on the robotic console, the chair was the weak link.

To solve the problem, I bought my own chair and kept its setting the same. This eliminated the chair as a variable. This adjustment—as well as others derived from the videotape—now lets me operate robotically for five to six hours a day with almost no pain.

The key to success, especially under pressure, is to eliminate and/or reduce as many variables as you can—to increase the reproducibility of your actions and of your team's actions. Recently I operated in India as a visiting professor in several different hospitals, teaching them new surgical techniques. I brought my own headlight, the surgical mask and hat that I am used to and that I wear every day in Birmingham at UAB, and even my own surgical shoes (clogs). This helped reduce my variables of operating in different countries and hospitals.

Back and neck pain are common injuries for surgeons, just as elbow and shoulder injuries are for pitchers. I was just getting out of the operating room on my way home when Robby called me. I could tell from his voice that something was seriously wrong. He had just finished an intrasquad scrimmage, and on the last pitch he heard a pop in his left elbow—his pitching elbow—and he knew it was serious.

A few days later, we found out that he had suffered an injury to his ulnar collateral ligament (UCL). Fortunately— after Robby saw Jimmy Andrews, probably the best-known orthopedic surgeon in the world, who lives right in my hometown of Birmingham—we found out that surgery was not needed. Dr. Andrews recommended intense rehabilitation.

Robby started his rehab immediately, the day after his injury. We then spent the next few days reviewing his pitching and throwing form carefully from my own videotapes of his games. We painstakingly studied his mechanics frame by frame, identified changes that he made with his new pitching coach, and immediately readjusted his mechanics. The careful videotape review and attention to his mechanics provided him with newfound confidence in his pitching, just as it did for me while I was learning to operate with the robot. Robby knew he would not get hurt now, and he was eager and excited to get back on the mound and reengage in the challenge of baseball. He worked hard to rehabilitate the injury, and very soon he was the team's number-one pitcher, throwing in the low nineties.

Physical injury is a part of life. We all get hurt and have injuries. Most of us—especially those of us who are older—rise out of bed every day with some ailment or ache or pain, and yet the vast majority of us go to work and work through it.

Once you get hurt, ask how you got hurt and see if you could have prevented it. Was it poor mechanics, poor judgment, or poor practice? Sometimes injuries are just unlucky, but that conclusion should be made last, and only after careful reflection. You should be willing to ask yourself whether any part of the injury was preventable and what you could have done to prevent it. Be willing to review everything you do, from driving a car to brushing your teeth to performing a robotic lobectomy. Even holding a pen or pencil incorrectly can injure your finger. If you have chronic pain from repeated motions that you perform at work, videotape yourself performing them and be willing to change those mechanics in order to get better.

The majority of chronic injures I see are from patients

being overweight (chronic back pain), emphysema from smoking, or liver disease from alcohol abuse. All of these are obviously preventable. Keep regular doctor appointments. Take care of your teeth and your eyes, and get screening tests like PSA and colonoscopy for men and mammography, PAP smears, and colonoscopy for women. These regularly scheduled tests usually help to prevent injuries and illnesses from becoming disabling ones.

The key to dealing with injuries is to have an attitude of wanting to immediately get better and reengage in your work. Each of us has a responsibility to want to return to our families and to society as productive members of both. American society has made it too easy for some with minor injuries to avoid going back to work. I have seen this in my clinic day after day, year after year: Thousands of Americans who could be working are on disability. They choose to accept a sick role.

But that sick role should be discouraged, not encouraged. After a chest operation, I tell my patients that they are no different than an injured athlete. They should immediately walk and participate in their own recovery. Obviously, as a physician, I know that some injuries, syndromes, and diseases make it impossible to return to full activity. But super performers deal with the daily aches and pains of life; they don't use physical ailments as excuses not to engage or to compete.

When you get injured, the sooner you reengage in the battle of life, the more you will respect yourself. Ask yourself when you are the happiest: after accepting a challenge and defeating the odds, or after surrendering and relaxing but watching from the bench?

It's an unfortunate fact that as we get older, our skills erode. Our muscles atrophy, our bones become more brittle, we get less flexible, and our vision and hearing becomes less acute. Exercise and a healthy diet help slow this erosion, but they do not prevent it. Thus we have to accept that these changes are just a part of life and growing older, and we have to understand that some of these changes are more likely to occur at different points in our careers. By anticipating these changes, you can adjust your mechanics to deal with them.

Your Response to Adversity Is What Defines You

I walked into my house on a Saturday afternoon with a bad feeling in the pit of my stomach, the feeling you get when you're ashamed of something you've done. I had just finished coaching a Little League basketball game. We had won, but I was ashamed of the way I had yelled at the referees and yelled at my players. What was worse: An older couple was sitting in the stands, watching their grandson play for the other team. I had operated on the husband a few years earlier, and after the game he came up to me and said that he was glad he had been under the care of such an "intense surgeon." But I knew he was just putting a positive spin on my poor behavior.

I made a promise to myself that day, sitting at home after

the game. I knew I could not control the referees—especially the ones that called games for eight- and nine-year-olds—but I *could* control my response.

And it started to work. One day, not long after, I was operating with a fairly new resident. I got around a large branch of the patient's pulmonary artery with a right-angle clamp and gently spread the clamp's jaws. We were around the artery perfectly. I showed the resident exactly how I wanted him to repeat the same movement and get the feel of getting around the vessel as well. He took the clamp from my hands and proceeded to tear a large hole in the pulmonary artery.

In the past, I would have yelled and told him he was an idiot, that he had endangered the life of a patient by taking an easy operation and making it hard. But, that Little League game on my mind, I tried to moderate my response to adversity. Instead of blaming him for the mistake, I looked at my role in the bad outcome. Maybe I could have provided him with a better angle or spent a few more seconds teaching him the subtleties of the surgical move. My response to adversity was finally maturing.

Too often when things go wrong, we are too quick to blame our teammates or colleagues at work. Even if the mistake was completely your colleague's fault and you're sure you had nothing to do with it, it's worth examining your role. Perhaps your lack of confidence in your colleague was a factor in his failure. Always ask yourself what you can do to make your teammates better. Consider taking responsibility for things you believe are out of your control, because they may not be.

And although many aspects of life really *are* out of your control, your response to these events is not. Learn from your previous responses to negative news that, in your judgment, were too emotional or uncontrolled. Understand how that response affects your performance and behavior right after you receive the news, and prepare a better response next time.

I have tried to inculcate this principle in my own three boys and in all the children I have coached over the years. However, I am now convinced that some skills cannot be developed until a certain age. It's almost a Piagetian type of skill development. However, adults should be able to learn this strategy. Proper execution first requires one to understand their response mechanism and then how to alter it. I now warn myself on the drive into work that I will not allow the typical operating-room delays and mistakes to affect my positive mood or positive interaction with others, especially those who work with me every day. This does not mean I will be kind to those who delay me or who continue to make mistakes, but my response is more tempered. I have learned to adapt what I say and do and focus more on how to positively influence those around me as opposed to reacting out of anger.

Unfortunately I have not been 100 percent true to my promise to control my response to adversity, but I have gotten a lot better since that day. We all have parts of our lives that we seem to have little or no control over. Some are minor—like referees in a basketball game—but some are major, like serious illnesses that are linked to our genetics, or just bad luck.

I thought of that as I placed my hand on Lorraine's leg while she dialed the phone to the doctor's office. She was calling to get the results of her breast biopsy done a few days earlier.

"It's cancer," the doctor said. My wife had breast cancer. I felt her body, which had been tight in anticipation, suddenly fade to one side of the chair. Her fingers loosened on my hand and slipped off.

But we had learned our lessons well: We knew that although we couldn't control the outcome of the report or her diagnosis, we could control our response. And so, before calling our three boys downstairs to tell them the news, we prepared ourselves for their possible responses, and how we would respond in turn to each.

CHAPTER 5

Getting and Staying in the Zone

Thinking Like a Super Performer

. . .

Blocking Out the Crowd Noise

The Zone

It was a Wednesday in June 2010—the day of Lorraine's mastectomy, with which I opened this book in the introduction. It was a typical day for me professionally. By that time, I had performed more thoracic operations per year (over a thousand a year for several years in a row) than probably anyone in the world. I had eight operations and three visiting surgeons who were observing our new surgical techniques and operating-room efficiency. But Lorraine's mastectomy made this day very different.

My first four operations, done in different operating rooms, were short and went well. My team and I were in the zone. Like a symphony, we performed as one. There were no delays getting in the operating rooms, there were no unnecessary surgical movements, and there was no bleeding.

The visitors were amazed. "You have done more operations already by nine thirty a.m. than I do in a whole week," one visiting surgeon said. My team and I hear this almost every day from our visitors. "Man, Cerf, you were in the zone the whole time."

That line rang a familiar bell in my mind. I had heard the exact same thing fifteen years ago from my opponent after I had just won a tennis tournament at a country club.

"Man, Cerf, you were in the zone the whole time," my opponent said as we shook hands across the tennis net. And he was right. I had raised my mental game, and I was able to slow down the pace of the game in my mind. I had limited the unforced errors that had often plagued me in the past. I played aggressively, and I dictated the play and the pace of the points. I was not afraid to go for my shots. I was willing to risk it and risk failure instead of playing it safe and being afraid to lose. I was in the zone the whole match.

The term *in the zone* is poorly understood and misinterpreted. Everyone has been in the zone, but many people treat it as an anomaly, a once-in-a-lifetime event. Instead, a professional can and should be able to get in the zone every day and stay there all day long. A professional gets in the zone more easily, stays there longer, and better understands why she is in it or why she is not in it than an amateur does. As a tennis player I never achieved that level, but as a surgeon, I have.

Importantly, when a professional is out of the zone, the lower limits of his or her performance are much closer to the zone than an amateur's performance. The range of play is much tighter, and the lows are not far away from the peak performance. This is a critical point. This is the key to being a professional. Even on your off days, few people should be able to tell that you are off. Each day you have to deliver at least an excellent level of play—and your outcomes must still be excellent.

Being in the zone for a super performer should not be a rare event; it should be an expected, even hackneyed occurrence. You should expect the zone of yourself and of your teammates from the first pitch to the last batter, from kickoff until the gun sounds, from tip-off until the horn sounds, from the opening incision on the first patient until the last closing suture on the last patient. Too often I hear sports announcers say, "Man, he is in the zone today." The reality is that we, as professional performers, should always be in the zone, every day, all day long. Most surgeons I know do this every day. The distractors of your pager going off, problems with patients on the floor, problems with the next patient checking in, emergency consults—all of these must be dealt with confidently and without interrupting the symphony of the operation that you are currently performing.

As a professional, you have to expect to immediately get in the zone as your day starts. Whether you are a surgeon or a stockbroker or a sports announcer, you should know your routine and allow it to set the triggers that get you in your high-performance zone each day. You have to set up a pregame routine, no matter what type of work you do. This will better allow you to get into the zone routinely. Moreover, it will help you get there on a day when you may have more pressure on you than usual, or when you are not feeling well.

Trust Your Pregame Routine

Recently my son Alec asked me what I was doing to get ready for an operation on a three-day-old that I had the next morning. He knew that it was a high-risk operation and that I was worried about it. I told him that I was following the same routine I followed every night and morning. I allowed my standard, well-rehearsed routine to keep my anxiety in check. This includes what you eat, when you work out, and how you sleep. It is your mind-set.

If getting in the zone for the day doesn't happen to you routinely, then your routine is wrong. You may be too rushed in the morning—if so, get up earlier. You may not feel prepared—if so, then prepare yourself better before you go to bed. Allow the routine itself to lead to improved anxiety management. If you trust the routine you devise, the routine itself will provide confidence that you are ready and will perform well. To achieve that level of trust, it's important to try to better understand which triggers and routine daily events get you into the zone and which ones make it harder for you to get in it and stay in it—and which ones cause you to fall out of it.

Just as getting in the zone has been vastly misinterpreted, so has staying in the zone. Staying in the zone is a by-product of your immersion in the task and in your performance. Distractors cannot remove you from it.

Anticipation is a key part of staying in the zone. When I am operating, I can literally see myself performing the next move before I do it. If you anticipate the next moves and see them in your mind's eye seconds before they occur, the zone becomes a movie rather than a series of still images. I did this in sports too, especially in fluid sports like football, hockey, baseball, and basketball, where you are reacting to an opponent's moves and you can predict what they are going to do at each instant. Your moves become fluid and a constant motion. Your physical actions actually become linked with your own breathing and heart rate. They become a part of you.

The analogy I use to explain this is possibly strange for someone who isn't a physician, but if you try to anticipate your actions while you're in the zone, it'll make intuitive sense. To stay in the zone, you need to make your skeletal muscles behave more like smooth muscles. Smooth muscle performs actions that occur involuntarily in our bodies. For example, our diaphragm is used for breathing, and parts of the esophageal muscle allow us to swallow food without our

active mental participation. By contrast, skeletal muscle—
such as the muscle in our arms and legs—controls our volun-
tary actions. When we perform, we're consciously using our
skeletal muscles. But to stay in the zone, we need to make our
skeletal muscle behave and react like smooth muscle. Make
these actions as routine and natural to you as breathing.

The Mind-Set of a Super Performer

When necessary distractors take your attention away for a
moment or two, immediately reset your pace and return to
your actions. All of us have random thoughts while we are
performing. Today I was thinking about my middle son and
whether or not he had sent out an important email while I
was getting around the pulmonary artery during a robotic
lobectomy. I did not beat myself up for "losing concentration,"
but rather chuckled quietly to myself as I easily and safely got
around the artery. It is normal to have thoughts or feelings
during critical parts of a performance that may not be related
to what you are doing. I have often told my trainees (my kids,
players I have coached, my surgical residents and fellows) that
many things will cross their minds during a performance—
maybe even during a critical time in that performance. This
is normal and okay—do not try to push positive thoughts.
The key is not to let those thoughts take you out of the zone.
Having them is fine; just recognize them and move on with
your performance.

Some thoughts will be negative. This is normal. Negative

thoughts during a game or operation are actually sometimes smart: "If I put a hole in that artery, this patient may die." That thought is correct; the patient may die from that mistake. "If I miss this putt, I may lose the golf tournament." That's correct; you might. It means you are aware of the consequence and of the magnitude of the moment.

I have too many young surgeons who want to try to control their thoughts at times of pressure. Some force themselves to think only positive thoughts. This sets them up for failure, because it is not human nature to have only positive thoughts. Sometimes your thoughts are random or unrelated to what you are doing. Sometimes your thoughts may even be negative. All of those thoughts are still okay. In fact, they might be just what you need at that time to perform well.

So allow your thoughts to happen and then refocus on the task at hand. Noticing someone or something in the crowd before a big moment in a game does not mean you are not ready to perform well. Thoughts merely exist; they do not determine your actions unless you let them.

In the movie *After Earth*, Will Smith's son is frightened. His dad states something similar to what I have been saying for a long time to many of the players I coached, to many of the residents I have taught, and to my three sons. There is a difference between being afraid or anxious and being aware that you are in danger or about to perform in a critical game. Fear and anxiety are emotions that only exist in your mind, and thus you are in control of them. However, knowing that danger exists or that this next action will affect the outcome of a particular major event is your heightened awareness of a surrounding moment. It shows alertness. It provides evidence that you are aware of surrounding danger. You know the consequence of making a mistake as opposed to being afraid of making a mistake. There is a big difference. You are not going to be 100 percent perfect—no one is; that is life.

One of the best ways of staying in the zone once you get there is to carefully take note of the experience. Immerse yourself in the visceral and mental aspect of what you are feeling when you are there. The novice will say that this may break you out of the zone and hurt your performance. But the reality is that the better you understand yourself and how you feel—and I mean exactly how you are feeling, including your breathing, your heart rate, your hand movements, your back and legs, and so on—the easier it is to get there and stay there. When I am operating, I've learned that a certain stance I have at the operating-room table helps me to immediately get in the zone. I position the operating bed just right, I have the patient turned just right, my headlight and magnifying glasses are positioned just right on my head. It is just like when I hit in baseball, and I always spread the dirt out in the batter's box just the way I like it.

Next time you are in the zone and playing well or operating well or speaking well or thinking crystal clear, ask yourself what exactly is happening that allows you to do this. What are the circumstances—is it a normal day, is there anything particularly pleasant or unpleasant about the room you're in, does your team seem to be performing better or worse than usual—and what did you do differently to prepare for this performance? As soon as the performance is over, write down everything about that experience—the feel, the smells, your heart rate, your thoughts, the tactile sensation, everything. How did it feel, and what were you doing during it and before it? What were you thinking? What is allowing you to perform so well at this time? The key to staying in the zone is to fully immerse yourself in what you are feeling while you are there.

The zone is just a physical and mental state where the mind and body are working as one in harmony, like a symphony. Learn to duplicate as much about that experience as you can in order to get there and stay there whenever you perform.

Blocking Out the Crowd Noise

I was on my eighth and final operation on the day of Lorraine's surgery, and it was by far the most difficult operation of the eight. I really wanted to finish this operation before Lorraine's operation was over so that I could be in the recovery room for her when she got out of the operating room.

The operation I was doing is called a pulmonary-artery sleeve resection of the left upper lobe. Despite its difficulty, I had considerable experience with this operation and had even written a chapter of a book and a paper on how best to perform it. Two of the three visiting surgeons who were there that day had come specifically to see how we set up and performed this operation.

And it was going well. I was still in the zone. One of the visitors commented on how deep the hole seemed, yet how I had barely spread the ribs apart with the chest retractor. "How can you operate through such a small incision?" the visitor asked. "Why not make it bigger and spread the rib retractor more, or even take a rib out? Especially for this large tumor."

I smiled subtly under my mask; I had heard this comment many times before. I now felt comfortable operating and performing through this small incision, even for a dangerous operation like this. I was on autopilot and in the zone. I even remember praying while I was performing the most critical part of the operation—which involved literally cutting the pulmonary artery in half—that the surgeon upstairs who was operating on my wife was in the zone that day too, and that Lorraine's sentinel lymph node would be benign.

And, as you've read in the introduction of this book, it wasn't: The sentinel lymph node was positive. Lorraine's cancer was not going to involve a simple mastectomy and a 95 percent cure rate. Lorraine's life had changed; our family's life had changed. Lorraine was a cancer patient. I was the husband of a cancer patient. Like so many patients and spouses that I saw and spoke to every day, we too would talk about chemotherapy. We too would worry every six months for what the CT scan that day would show. We too would pray that the tests were "all clear." We too would think silently about mortality.

I turned my attention back to the operative field, but I was in some sort of shock. For the first time in my life, I couldn't do the operation. The hole I had been smirking about just minutes before now looked incredibly deep. It was a bottomless abyss, dark, cold, and dangerous. "How do I operate in such a small and dark hole?" I asked myself as my confidence ran away. The instruments aren't even long enough to reach down there. How was I going to perform in such a hostile environment? I considered calling one of the several surgeons who are always available as backup during our operations.

My mind took me back to another hostile environment during college baseball. "Hey, Seven, what's your problem, Seven? Why are you looking up in the stands? You've got rabbit ears." Earlier in the game, I had chased a foul ball down the left-field line from my shortstop position, and I ran into the fence. My glove went into the crowd, and I cut my nose. A security guard had to retrieve my glove from some of the intoxicated fans who were drinking beer while sunning their bare chests. They had been dogging me ever since.

Those are just words, I told myself, just words. Words and sounds have no influence on the speed of the baseball or its movement. They do not and cannot affect how fast their pitcher pitches or how I see or react to that pitch. They cannot affect how I play ball. And true enough, I went three for four at the plate that day.

I told myself the same thing again: What Lorraine's surgeon had said were just words. Words could not affect my performance in any way. They couldn't affect my surgical field or my vision or my ability to operate unless I let them. Just as I had done in that ball game—roped a double in the gap with the bases juiced—I would overcome these words and perform. I had to: My patient was counting on me to get him out of the operating room safely. I should be able to deal with this, given all the training I had done for blocking out crowd noise.

As I've described, I sometimes use extraneous noise and interruptions intentionally when I lead teams through practice. I used to yell horrible things to my kids in my backyard as they practiced free throws. I used to trash-talk them when they were six, seven, eight years old whenever we played baseball or whenever we competed in any event, even during board games. When we played Ping-Pong, I did everything I could to distract them mentally. Then, later, I would review how they handled my verbal assault and what strategies they used to ignore me. It helps to practice being interrupted and upset. It's like when LeBron James addressed his "haters" during his 2013 playoff run: "I can't worry about what anyone says about me." Those playoffs ended with his second ring. Don't allow the crowd, the media, or anyone to affect your performance.

Adapting to Field Conditions

Although crowd noise during your presentation or boos as you shoot a free throw cannot affect your performance unless you allow them to, field conditions can. If the screen does not come all the way down for your presentation or the light bulb is dull, if the athletic field is wet and the ball is slick, all of these will affect your performance in a way you can't control. So you have to be prepared to adapt to different field conditions, which means you have to have carefully considered all of the possible field conditions that exist. For example, when I traveled to Europe, Asia, or India to operate and lecture, their customs were quite different, and I needed to learn them long before the trip.

In lung cancer surgery, the operative field often changes for the worse. Obese patients make the operation much more difficult: The ribs are closer together, and longer instruments are required. Radiation prior to surgery can also dramatically change our playing field. Some patients' lungs move up and down more during surgery, or their hearts move more often. We have to adjust to the gyration and operate on a moving target. These are the changing field conditions for a surgeon, much like a soggy field, poor lighting, or long grass for an athlete.

You have to practice in or anticipate the different field conditions in order to be ready to perform in them all. If you are a football player, you should have several different-length spikes for your cleats. If you are a businessperson and the venue of a meeting might change or the clients' tastes change for that night, you have to be able to predict this in order to be adaptable and change on the go. In Birmingham, whenever the weather got below forty degrees, I used to make my kids hit in our batting cage.

"Gentlemen," I told them. "We are blessed today with a great opportunity. It is cold. Let's go out to the batting cage and simulate baseball-playoff weather in the northeast."

Field conditions are one thing, but the news of Lorraine's lymph node had not changed my playing field: It was only words from a hostile crowd.

Strategies for Relaxation

I thought that, having gone over that hostile baseball game in my mind, I would have to overcome my anxiety, as I'd done so many times before. And so I turned my attention back to the operative field. It was just a brief moment, and Lorraine's surgeon was still standing there and had just started to turn to walk out of the operating room. Everything was moving in slow motion. What I thought had been a minute while I was mentally incompetent turned out only to be a split second. Surely I would be fine.

And yet, when I looked back into the operative field, I still saw it as an insurmountable foe. When else in my life had I experienced this, and how had I responded? The patient depended on me, and I tried to think.

It was the final of the New Jersey state Ping-Pong tournament, and I was eleven years old. It was 1973. The venue was not a stadium but an old high school gym packed full of parents and players who'd stuck around to watch the final match. As the game started, I remember going to serve but feeling tight inside, uneasy. I was so nervous that for those first few points of the first game, I literally had a tiny tremor to my hands. I played tentatively and was not going for or hitting my shots. More importantly, I was afraid to go for winners. At the time, I hadn't yet developed any strategies to relax myself. I had no mental exercise to calm myself down. In my mind it was the finals of Wimbledon instead of a meaningless junior Ping-Pong tournament in an old dilapidated gym.

I lost the match, and lost the state championship, mainly because of my inability to play well under pressure. If only I had prepared how to relax myself, I probably would have won. But now, in the operating room, I *had* learned to relax myself and had developed mental techniques to better prepare. I had learned my lesson from that game. Why weren't those strategies working?

I remembered one of the first times I very consciously employed my strategies for relaxation. It was my first collegiate at bat. I stepped out of the batter's box and took a few deep breaths. I slowed down my heart rate and my breathing and imagined myself totally relaxed, hitting in the batting cage on a beautiful sunny day. I gripped the bat as hard as I could with my hands and then felt my muscles let go as I let them completely relax. I saw myself as if I were sitting in the press box and pretended to announce myself coming up to the plate. I visualized myself from several different vantage points: the press box, the pitcher's mound, the third base coaches' box. I slowed everything down in my mind, and the action in front of me went in slow motion as well. At last I managed to conquer my nervousness; I was ready. I was completely relaxed and confident, and on the first pitch, I lined a two-seam cut fastball for a base hit.

And so, in the operating room that day, I started to employ all of the relaxation techniques that I had inculcated in myself as a high school and college athlete, the techniques that I had taught to my three boys and the hundreds of athletes, medical students, residents, and fellows I had trained how to perform under pressure. I focused my eyes on an inanimate object—in this case, it was a clamp on the blue sterile towels that hung around the operative field—just as I had done using home plate when I was hitting in a big baseball game. I took a few deep breaths to relax, to refocus, to live in the moment, and I squeezed my hands to let them totally relax. I visualized myself from my own vantage point operating smoothly and calmly, and then I visualized myself from afar, as if someone else was filming me. I visualized myself from my hands, as if they had a camera on them, and then from an overhead camera watching myself. I even started positive self-talk: "Remember, you are the best, no one is better than you; you have done this operation a hundred times; you wrote a chapter on this operation; you teach people how to do this . . ."

There are many strategies to relax under pressure. Here's a partial list:

- controlling your breathing
- visualizing yourself from different viewpoints (such as yours, the opponent's, the crowd's, and even from the perspective of the scalpel or the ball)
- seeing the field in slow motion
- engaging in positive self-talk
- recalling previous success
- trusting your muscle memory to take over
- staying in the present
- keeping it simple—not overthinking your body's moves
- limiting your self-anger when you make a mistake; being more forgiving at the time
- learning from your mistakes during the contest
- seeing each passing moment of the game or operation as a new challenge—forget whether or not you lost the challenge a moment ago, then reset and focus on the next one coming up

Many books and seminars have been devoted to the precise manner in which to employ these strategies. But the key is to find the one that works for you and then instill it in your practice, even when you are not nervous. Practice using it again and again, and then when you need it, the strategy itself can take over via muscle memory. Too few performers actually try to practice these strategies, and thus too few become super performers.

Visualization

Visualization—as I used to prepare for Anna's operation in chapter 2—is one of my key strategies. A lot has been written about visualization. We all have seen Olympic skiers on top of the mountain just before their Olympic run at history. Many close their eyes, sway their bodies, and wave their arms back and forth as if they were actually skiing the slalom course in their mind's eye. This kind of visualization can be done with any act in which the opponent does not change (e.g., a ski slope or a bowling alley).

However, if you have to adjust to a competitor (as in baseball, basketball, or surgery, when you encounter a chest containing different-size cancers), your visualization techniques must change. It still helps to visualize yourself competing and interacting, but you have to factor in the changing field conditions, including your opponent's movements and adjustments to your actions. I prefer then to visualize myself from my own eyes, as I would see my competitor, rather than as an observer watching myself compete from a vantage point.

When using visualization, try to picture yourself in your mind's eye as totally calm and confident. See yourself performing during past victories with total calmness and confidence. Feel and see yourself being successful both before the game and during it. Feel how calm you were in practice the day before, when you were doing the exact same thing you're doing now. Feel the swagger from within yourself because you know you can do it and do it well. Through visualization, you can apply that feeling to the current situation.

Visualization allows you to relax and let your muscle memory take over. Some call this process allowing your body to take control of your mind, or preventing your mind from getting in the way of the body. We all intuitively understand this analogy, but I've never liked it: Your brain should always be in control of your body and your actions. But you do have to know when to trust your muscle memory and your pre-game or pre-act routine, especially when under pressure.

As we've discussed before, visualization is easier if you have someone film you while you perform. Then you are able to see yourself as others see you. Professional athletes have a distinct advantage because most of their games are filmed in high-definition film and from many different camera angles, but you can bring similar techniques to your own preparation.

Another way to visualize is to actually visit the arena or the area in which you are going to perform. Take pictures along the way, including where you are going to park and the walk to the field itself. If you are playing a big game, get pictures of the locker room you will be in and the ramp you will walk up to enter the field. If you are going to give an important speech, go to the meeting hall the night before if you can. Take pictures of the podium and of the stairs you will have to climb to get on stage. Familiarize yourself with the lectern or podium and play with the microphone, the slide advancer, etc. Then, later that night, review those pictures. This will take some of the uncertainty and unfamiliarity out of the experience and thereby reduce the stress.

The day before Matthew's first pro baseball tryout, we got to the hotel late at night, and—despite his resistance— immediately drove to the baseball park twenty-five minutes away. We found out exactly how to get there. We walked the infield and learned the lip of the infield grass and the bounces the ball might take. After the tryout, he said that this late-night journey had helped him dramatically. By visualizing the field of competition, he was able to feel comfortable in it and allow his muscle memory to take over.

Keep It Simple

Here in the operating room, staring into the deep, dark chest, all of my visualization techniques had failed me. I considered calling for another surgeon to come help me, but he would be a good ten minutes out. Was I really going to just sit here and wait and do nothing until then? No, the patient came first, so I asked the nurse to call to see if my partner was around.

The patient was safe and doing well, and the pulmonary artery was clamped. Ten more minutes of anesthesia would not hurt. But suppose the worst happened and the surgeon I'd called couldn't make it on time. Suppose a bleed started while we were waiting. Waiting ten minutes seemed less and less like a reasonable option.

I knew I had to face my fears for the patient's sake. I asked for the needle driver and the suture. But as soon as I had a hold of them and began to bring them into the operative field, I realized that my hands were on the verge of trembling. My usual skill and confidence were not there. I had never really been in a situation like this in the operating room as an attending surgeon, where my mind was preventing my body from doing a skill I had done many times in the past. I had not really prepared for how I was going to react to this disaster.

But I had always prepared for everything, even for coaching Little League baseball. Once, as a baseball coach, I told the umpires before the game started that we had developed a few trick plays. It was important to me, I stressed, that the umpires knew that these plays were legal and not to be scored as balks by the pitcher. Believe it or not, you can get umpires to listen to you if you address them nicely.

As the game moved on, it was 6–5, and we were ahead in the last inning of the finals of an all-star baseball tournament. Our pitcher had just walked two batters in a row to load the bases. He was tired. There were two outs, but their best hitter was coming up. I had no one left in relief. I calmly stepped out of the dugout and gave the verbal cue to my team for the trick play.

"There are two outs, full count, bases are juiced, the

runners are going on the pitch—infielders, the play is at first." And then I took my hat off and rubbed my forehead.

The kids knew the signal; we had practiced it enough times before, and even the umpires knew it was coming and that it was legal. The pitcher stood on the back of the rubber and pretended to go into a windup. However, he stepped off with the other foot. The base runners, having missed the step-off, had already started to run, thinking the pitcher was going to home plate. Instead, he threw the ball to the third baseman, putting the runner in a rundown. We tagged him out to win the game.

The opponent's fans went ballistic, yelling that it was illegal, it was a balk, it was a trick, it was unfair. But no, it was baseball. We had prepared this play for just such a disaster situation: a fatigued pitcher who couldn't count on his usual skill to bring in the win. I had prepared my team to perform even in a situation when they literally couldn't perform. And I had prepared the umpires before the game so that they would not call a balk.

You cannot prepare for everything. Some disasters and some errors are just unavoidable—not many, but some. And although we cannot prevent all of the disasters or unforeseen circumstances in life, we can prepare our reaction to those disasters no matter what they are.

One good way to do this is to tell yourself exactly how you are going to stay calm and collected, no matter what happens today during the operation, game, meeting, event, etc. Write down exactly how you are going to respond to whatever adversity shows up on your doorstep.

Sometimes, although we do not want to think about it, we can fall out of the zone in the middle of a game, an event, or a performance. When this happens, only one response is possible: Keep it simple.

Sometimes, you first have to truly understand the complexities involved in a system or in a process in order to be able to simplify it. For example, when I was a first-year cardiothoracic surgeon, I quickly learned that when sewing a bypass graft to a coronary artery, you have to place about ten to twelve tiny stitches using sutures as small in width as a human hair. A suture that is just one millimeter off can mean the difference between a patient walking home or having a massive heart attack after surgery. In other words, the finest details and intricacies make the difference in outcome for operations in the chest. These details seem trivial to the casual or uninitiated observer. However, to a professional who is immersed in the field every day, these tiny details separate the super performers from the average performers.

Thus, all of the intricacies of a situation need to be reviewed during practice. Ensure that each team member knows all of the intricacies, but also remind them that during the game, when things start to go poorly, they must know how to reduce the process to its simplest terms. Allow the autopilot to take over, trust your muscle memory, and keep it simple.

In the operating room that day, I gave myself that same advice again that I've told to others on many occasions: Thoracic surgery seems very complex and complicated to most. But like a consistent golf swing, it can be broken down into a set of very simple moves. When things are going wrong or the momentum shifts against you, I often tell the resident, "Just keep it simple, stupid." When you walk out to the mound and a pitcher is struggling with his control, the worst thing you can do is to start to talk about his mechanics and tell him that his shoulder is open, he is stepping open, his arm is too high, etc. All you'll do is paralyze him with physical corrections. It is better to tell him to relax, slow down, and just play catch with the catcher and throw strikes. Simple. If I was going to complete this operation, keeping it simple was going to be a critical cog for a positive outcome.

CHAPTER 6

The Game Must Go
On, and with Humility

The World Keeps Spinning

. . .

Winning Without Your "A" Game

Know When to Bench Yourself

As I grabbed the needle driver from the nurse and started sewing the pulmonary artery back together again, the words that one of my visitors said began to ring in my ears again: Why was I operating today with Lorraine having surgery for breast cancer?

Maybe I should not have been here. Maybe I should have taken the day off like most everyone else would have. I could be sitting in the waiting room just praying for good news. But I had never done that. Like most super performers, I had never missed a day of work or surgery for my patients. When Matthew had almost drowned in our swimming pool the night before, I did all eight patients on my operating-room schedule that day. When my dad had open-heart surgery while I was a fellow at Mayo, I operated in the room right next door. Likewise, I did not miss surgery when Robby was born. I ran to the operating room to be on time. I did not miss operating when my mom had open-heart surgery while I was an attending surgeon at UAB. I operated right next door to her in my own operating room and did ten operations that day. I did not miss surgery when I broke my rib, tore my meniscus, tore my labium, or had the flu.

Most surgeons show up to work every day, because we have an intense responsibility to our patients. I was no different. But, maybe there is a time when you should not show up to compete. Maybe there is a time when you need to recognize that you, your team, and your patients are all better off without you that particular day.

As super performers, we should be smart enough to recognize these days, to know our limitations and when to bench ourselves. Maybe this, for me, was one such day. But it was too late: I was already in the arena and deep in the middle of the game.

Good or bad, I had inculcated this same culture into my children, as Robby illustrated all too well in June 2013.

It was a beautiful, sunny Saturday afternoon when I heard Robby's name called on ESPN draft coverage. "The Los

Angeles Dodgers select Rob Cerfolio, pitcher from Yale from Indian Springs, Alabama." I texted Robby to let him know because he had to leave his TV set to get ready to pitch. He was in the bullpen warming up for a start for the Mankato MoonDogs in Minnesota in the Northwoods League. It was fitting that he was practicing his trade when he got drafted into Major League Baseball.

His ankle had been sore for a week or so at that point, but he'd told me that it was not that bad. I suggested that maybe he should not pitch tonight since he had just been drafted and it might affect his signing. We could check out his ankle, make sure it was fine, and then decide whether he should return for his senior year at Yale or go to rookie ball. But he decided to pitch that night because, like most super performers, he loves to compete.

In the third inning, the batter Robby faced hit a humpback soft liner over his head. Robby dove back and made an incredible catch on the back part of the mound. However, potentially due to the previous injury, he fractured his ankle. But he just kept pitching and competing, although the injury caused him to give up three runs over the next three innings.

The Dodgers' organization was as honest and up front with us as we were with them. Since his rehabilitation would take three to four months and since rookie ball would be over by that time, it made no sense to sign him. He would go back to Yale, complete his senior year while pitching, get his degree, finish his premed program, and reenter the draft in 2014.

Perhaps he should not have pitched that night. Perhaps he should have taken the night off and not competed. There are times when it may be best to decide not to compete, but these times should be exceedingly rare. Too many Americans unfortunately overplay the "I can't come in today" card and find it too easy to bench themselves and stay home from work. A super performer wants to engage, but a super performer should also know when his performance may be worse for the team than no performance at all.

Lorraine, my three children, and I had created a culture around ourselves, our family, and our work environment of being mentally and physically tough. Creating such a culture, as we've talked about, doesn't mean that you deny yourself the proper care of your body and mind or do not take vacations. These events are needed, and a leader who plays the martyr at work only sets a negative tone of martyrdom that doesn't lead to high-quality results at work or at home. By playing the martyr, a leader teaches his team that it is right to purposely deny yourself the good things in life.

I am proud of the fact that I have not missed one day of work for illness in twenty-five years of being an MD. But I do not deny myself good medical care. Americans still value dedication of this kind, as we saw with the public celebration of Cal Ripken when his consecutive-games-played streak finally came to an end. However, there are times when you have to be honest with yourself and know that you cannot perform as well as you should. Maybe it is best for you, your teammates, and your patients if you do not show up.

If you do face a situation in which it's better to bench yourself, you must ensure that your teammates are aware of your pending absence well in advance if possible. The work must still get done. You, as a super performer and leader, have to ensure that someone can cover for you and take over all of your responsibilities. Your responsibilities do not magically disappear just because you cannot complete your work that day.

"The world keeps spinning," as I often remind my residents; the game must go on whether you are perfect this day or not. Whether you have a day off, a break, or have to go home before work is done because of the new residency hour restrictions enacted by our government, our responsibilities to others still exist and must be honored. You are still responsible for getting them not just done, but completed with a high level of quality. Super performers find a way to get all of their responsibilities done, and done well.

Super Performing When You Don't Have Your "A" Game

Maybe I should not have operated the day my wife was having her surgery. But there I was, knee-deep in a big operation. That decision was already made. Once you decide to compete, you have to give 100 percent. There is no casual effort in surgery or in life.

And slowly, my training took over. I told myself that I was fine, Lorraine would be fine, our family would be fine. We always were, and we always found a way to win. There was no news that we could not handle together as a family, including Lorraine's cancerous sentinel lymph node.

I grabbed the needle driver and started to sew. "I have to get tougher," I said out loud, but only loud enough for me to hear inside my surgical mask. I got super determined.

It was not pretty at first. My sewing was a bit shaky, slow, and tentative. But the first stitch was not that bad. The next stitch was slightly better, and then slowly, after a few seconds my skill started to return. *I can do this*, I said to myself. *I'm Robert J. Cerfolio, and I can do this better than anyone in the world.*

Most importantly, even if not true, I really believed that to be true with all my heart and soul. I may not have felt great, but I was going to deliver a win for this patient. He deserved it. He deserved for his surgeon to be a professional who delivered a certain product, irrespective of how his personal life was going or how he felt that day.

Surgeons are like athletes. We have to perform well even when we're not feeling well or when extraneous factors are working against us. Michael Jordan had a fever of 103 degrees during one of the 1997 NBA championship-series games. Yet Jordan, as a super performer, put up a thirty-eight-point performance, and the Bulls won that game and went on to win that series and another ring.

There will be many days when you just do not feel your best. I had a surgeon tell me one day that he could tell in the morning while he was scrubbing his hands just before his first case if he was going to be good that day or not. We all know what he means. There are days when a professional pitcher climbs the hill in the bullpen and can tell immediately that he just does not have his best fastball or best slider that day. But as a professional athlete, as a super performer, he still has to deliver a high-quality start. But more significantly, we as super performers need to tell our hands that we are going to be good today; we need to determine how we perform.

We all have to find a way to deliver a certain high level of performance on days when we are just a bit off. As a super performer, you have to find a way around your mediocrity. Your product, even though it may not be *your* best, has to be better than your opponent's best. You have to find a way to get the tumor out without losing any blood. If you have not fought through adversity and practiced your trade on days when you do not feel well, you will not be able to deliver under pressure on similar days. Maybe you run a business and had a poor night's sleep or problems at home. It does not matter. You need to show up and get your job done with a high level of competence.

You will never be able to perform under pressure on days you do not feel well if you have not practiced on days when you feel ill. I have always encouraged my athletes to show up for practice on days when they feel "a bit" sick. How else can you perform on game day feeling poorly unless you have practiced when feeling ill?

Keep Shooting

As I kept sewing up the artery, I slowly felt my dexterity returning. The act itself had helped me regain my confidence. I just kept sewing, and I was getting a bit better with each stitch. I even had positive self-talk going. This is something I had never even used in the operating room before, but I had in sports many times. I needed it now in the operating room.

"Keep shooting!" I had yelled once as I watched my son Alec miss shot after shot in one of our basketball games. I required that same mentality in the operating room: People couldn't be afraid to fail. I was sewing a fragile artery coming out of the right side of the heart, not shooting a basketball. But I kept telling myself, *Keep shooting—keep sewing.* And it was working. Sometimes, just like a good shooting guard who is in a slump and needs to shoot his way out of it, I needed to sew my way out of it. And I did.

I could feel the calmness drip down my shoulders. This is another technique, one I taught myself while playing shortstop in college. In my first two years of college baseball, I made too many errors at short. But in my last two years, I became more consistent. I learned not to rush. My cadence became smoother and my internal clock more accurate when it came to calculating the time I had to field and throw to first to just nip the runner. Part of the reason for that success was the image I created of a bottle of calmness that I could open up just prior to each inning. I could "pour some calmness" down my head and let it gently run down onto my shoulders and down my arms. This image soothed me like warm water in the shower. Now, in the operating room, I did the same. I poured some calmness down my shoulders onto my hands. It helped soothe me and took my mind far away from the news of Lorraine's lymph node.

I was wearing a camera that was mounted on my headlight. This provided our surgical visitors with a perfect magnified view of everything I was doing in incredible detail as they watched on a large monitor in the operating room. I started to announce my strategy with each stitch. "I like to start the anastomosis here," I pointed out. "This way the knot is kept off of the pericardium, and it's prevented from eroding into the heart over time." I announced my actions as I worked, stitch by stitch. This strategy also helped me to disconnect my mind from my body in a way and put my skills on autopilot. I used my cognitive understanding of what I was doing, almost as if I were teaching another person how to do it. This is another technique I borrowed from athletics: Sometimes when I competed in sports in college, I would announce the game to myself as I played. My verbalization of what I was doing and the reasons why I was doing it helped to remove me from myself in a way. Now, explaining my actions to the visitors made it easier and easier for me to sew. One visitor said, "I do not know how you can sew this well after getting this news about your wife." This gave me further confidence to keep going.

It seemed like hours since I had lost the ability to perform, but it had only been a second or two. Now I could feel the calmness running down my neck, onto my shoulders, and down my arms into my hands and fingertips. I was sewing well, and my confidence was back to normal. I could feel the warm swagger and calmness surrounding the very end of my fingers as I cut and sewed and tied. I was back. I was back on my game—back in the zone.

Pinnacle Performance

I finished that operation with a newfound grace and speed. By the end of it, I found that I had reached an even higher level of performance than I had just a few days ago. Perhaps the near epic failure that I had experienced just minutes earlier had helped to propel me to a new level technically and mentally as a surgeon. I do not know. Or perhaps it was just my burning desire to get to the recovery room to be there before Lorraine woke up from her anesthesia. I wanted her eyes, when they first opened, to see my face.

My patient did well. His cancer was completely re-moved, and we spared his left lower lobe. It was a win-win for everyone.

There were other changes as well. During the closure, one

of the residents, who was still learning the very basics of sewing, was struggling with the final stitches. Normally, I would have been harsh with him for not being able to perform a closure that seemed incredibly simple to me, but today, I was remarkably more humble toward him, and I spoke to him in a much more patient tone than the one I usually used. Because now I was a surgeon who understood that my skill could, at any moment, be lost. I too was vulnerable to losing it all. This concept was something I had not even considered as possible just thirty minutes earlier.

This was the most important thing I learned about myself that day. Despite all of my experience and success in sports and in the operating room; despite having been a first-team Academic All-American in baseball; despite having performed over fourteen thousand operations as an attending surgeon; despite all the coaching I had done and all the residents I had taught; despite all of my previous successes, awards, and operative experience I had gathered; despite all the lessons I had learned from all of my previous losses and the level at which I had learned to perform, I could still lose it all in a moment. I was still a weak, carbon-based life-form. Despite all of the tough experiences that had molded me into a seasoned performer, I was still disappointingly fragile.

It is this realization that draws the aging athlete to continue to play. It is his fear of losing this ability to come through again and again at the critical moments that pushes him back to the arena and further away from retirement. *Do I still have it?* they ponder. *Can I still get it done well at crunch time?* It is the thrill of the challenge, the competition itself, that draws us as surgeons and as athletes back to the arena. That is why so many surgeons and aging athletes find it so hard to retire.

As soon as we had closed, I asked the resident to talk to the family first, and I ran up to the recovery room to see Lorraine. I got up there before she completely came to. She was still groggy, but when she opened her eyes, my face was the first she saw. (Maybe this is why she had so much post-op nausea later that day.)

I did not want to tell her about the lymph node just yet. I thought it best that I get the boys into the hospital so that we could all tell her together as a family. So I called home and told my boys—coldly and matter-of-factly—that their mother's sentinel lymph node had cancer in it. In retrospect, a phone conversation was not the best way to do this, but unfortunately that is what I did. I told them to immediately drive into the hospital and get into her room so we could all tell her together.

By the time my boys got there, Robby had already Googled the five-year survival rate for a T1N1M0 adenocarcinoma of the breast. It was 87 percent, and I was elated. They wheeled Lorraine into the room and transferred her to her bed. I sat on the bed and took her hand in the same manner I had done for thousands of patients I had been required to tell after surgery that they had cancer—only this time it was my wife of twenty years.

My three boys stood behind me standing tall and proud as I told her that the sentinel lymph node was positive. She started to cry. "What . . . how could it be? The breast cancer was only a nine-millimeter lesion," she lamented. Her tears and her style of crying were so much like her—quiet, humble, and unassuming, but so incredibly vulnerable. "Does this mean I have to get chemo—what does that mean?" She started to cry again.

"Yes," I said, "probably, but let's wait and see what the final path shows. But whatever it shows and whatever you have to do, we will get through it together." And then I repeated what I had told her every night for twenty years of marriage when we lay in bed before going to sleep: "I love you, wifey, I will always love you, and I will always be here for you." That day this familiar daily line resonated a bit louder.

I had not seen my sons cry from emotions before, only from injuries they had suffered when they were younger, a long time ago. But now, all three had tears in their eyes. Robby, my oldest, turned his head toward the window to hide his tears. Alec teared up silently and gave Lorraine a hug, and Matthew placed his head on her chest. Robby peered out the window and gazed outside to view his new future. Perhaps as a family we realized what I had in that operating room that day. We were not perfect; we did not live in Camelot. We could lose it all quickly, and our life could change—as it had—in an instant.

Earlier in my career, after I had finished a particularly difficult operation or an operation on a VIP, I would congratulate myself on a job well done. But more recently over the past several years, I learned to congratulate my team more publicly and thank the good Lord for the good outcome. The sooner you realize that a big win only means that a new challenge is coming up the very next day, the more humble you will be. For a surgeon, it comes in a matter of a few minutes as the next patient is wheeled into the operating room. If you are a businessperson, it may be a few weeks before you get to close the next lucrative deal or close the deal that bankrupts the company. If you are an athlete and just won a ring, it may be several months before the next game comes—but it is coming. No matter how long it takes, another challenge is coming. There will be another time when you will be under intense pressure to perform, and your outcome may not be as favorable.

So enjoy your win, but enjoy it briefly. Realize you may fail the next day—or, in a surgeon's case, in the next few minutes. You should allow each win to make you a bit stronger, smarter, and more experienced, but still try to stay humble with each one.

This isn't always easy: I have had a few athletes and surgeons who I had to tell to go into a bathroom by themselves, look in the mirror, and scream and yell with joy, but then to compose themselves and check their joy at the door before talking to the press or telling the family that the cancer is out and their loved one is fine.

Ego needs to be put into perspective. Give credit to your team and to God for your talent and for the opportunity to have the challenge. The momentary loss of my ability to operate made me not only more humble and vulnerable, but somehow stronger and better as well; in part, this is because I realized that the chance to compete—which can vanish in a moment—is the biggest gift of all.

CHAPTER 7
Pressure Equals Opportunity

Keeping Family Connections

. . .

Shrinking the Lines of the Playing Field

Home Field Advantage

I spent the night after Lorraine's mastectomy in the hospital with her, and I slept by her side in her room. My boys were at home on their own. Lorraine and I got up early and had breakfast together. I grabbed a quick shower in the call room, gave a lecture to a set of four new visitors who had flown in the night before, and by the time I came back to see her at 6:50 a.m. before my operations were to start, two of her best friends, Jan and Nanette, were already there in her room taking shifts so she would never be alone.

I did well all day, performing ten operations. There seemed to be no residual effects from yesterday's problems. After my operations were over, I saw Lorraine briefly. During the visit, I reminded her that I had to catch a flight to Chicago that afternoon: I had a lecture at nine p.m. at a restaurant, and then a lecture at a Chicago hospital for grand rounds at six thirty a.m. the next morning, and then I was back home— one of my typical sub-twenty-four-hour trips. Lorraine was not happy that I was flying out of town on the first day after her operation. But these lectures had been scheduled over nine months ago, and many people, doctors, and nurses were counting on me to show up. I did not want to cancel on them. I had a responsibility to them, and now I knew that Lorraine was okay and recovering well. I told her I would be back before she knew it.

For the next eighteen hours, Lorraine's friends set up shifts to ensure that she was never alone, and they slept with her in the hospital room. This is a common tradition in the South. Lorraine had some of the best friends a person could possibly know—the best way to have great friends is to be one, and she was.

My lecture went fine, and I flew back to Birmingham from Chicago and ran to the operating room. I had only three operations in the afternoon, and I operated well all that day and the next. I was at incredible peace. And I noted that I operated better and was more at peace when I was operating with my surgical team at home than when operating with another team on the road. Sleeping in the hospital by Lorraine's side also gave me a new insight into what patients go through. The logistics of sleeping in the hospital and hanging on every word the doctors said—I understood now the complete vulnerability patients had to their doctors, the nurses, and the entire hospital setting. They needed us for everything: food, water, even clothing. They were completely dependent on us for life. It was something I'd always known to some degree, but I hadn't really understood on an immediate level before this time.

As soon as the day was over, I ran back up to Lorraine's room. "Here I am, back at your side, and in less than twenty-four hours." I was finally back home.

Why does home-field advantage matter so much in so many sporting events? What is it about having a supportive crowd that helps one set of players beat another? Is it just familiarity with the court, or getting to sleep in your own bed, or is it more? Does having your friends, family, and support system close by matter that much, and has this advantage changed over the years as athletes have become mentally tougher?

The answers to all of these questions depend on your mindset. All I know is that my feelings of increased connection to Lorraine during her operation made me perform significantly better under pressure than I had perhaps in years. My feelings of connection also helped me improve the performance of others around me.

Staying Connected to Your Family

A few months ago, I was operating with a resident who was particularly nervous. She was quite tremulous and unable to sew. She was used to operating in the abdomen, which is a very different type of surgery than being in the chest and operating on the heart and lungs: For many surgeons used to abdominal surgery, going from the one area of the body to the other can be like playing on the road in a noisy, unfriendly stadium. It was no different with this resident: She was very shaky and extremely nervous. I knew that her hands were good and that she had the technical ability to do some of this operation, but that her mind was preventing her from performing.

She had just delivered her first child a few months ago. I gently touched her hand with mine and held it for a brief moment. I asked her to just imagine herself lying on her bed at home later that night and to imagine that her newborn baby was falling asleep on her belly.

"Picture her beautiful face and her calm innocence as she falls asleep in your arms," I suggested. "She and your husband are going to unconditionally love you tonight, no matter how you do right now, no matter how you sew that lung, no matter how much you shake. It is okay for them—your performance right now does not matter to them."

She refocused and got a little better. It was not perfect, but it was better.

So I continued, as she gradually shook less and less and

became as fully competent as I knew she could be: "This operation is eventually going to end. This patient is going to do great, and you will be home soon enough, completely relaxed. Your family will love you. But you will be left alone with your thoughts and your knowledge of how well you did or did not perform. Only you will really know if you approved of how well you performed today. Only you will really know if you meet your preconceived expectation that you had set for yourself in today's operation with me. So let's have fun now and meet your expectation of what you and I both know you can do right now."

I, like most people, am happiest at work when I have performed well and treated my team members well. I feel incredibly fulfilled when I have finished a tough operation, been kind and patient with my teammates and residents in the operating room (which is still, unfortunately, too rare), and then spent quality time with the patient's family members after surgery.

One night after such a day, I was walking across the street on the way to my car. It was eight thirty at night, and I was finally on my way home. An elderly woman was lost and trying to find her way into the hospital. I took the time to walk her all the way over to the admitting area. When I finally arrived home, my wife commented that I was in an especially good mood for having had such a long day in the operating room and coming home so late at night.

While you're under pressure, it's important to stay

connected to people. A good sports example of this is tennis. It is common for the best players in the world to look into their families' and coaches' box for emotional support, especially during championship matches. In addition, if you can stay connected to other humans, even some you do not know well can provide you comfort and happiness. The human relationship I formed with a stranger that I will never see again was a strong example of this. It was totally irrelevant to her that I had performed surgery that day—she was just happy I helped her find her way to the front door.

But family is best, because family—usually—are among the few people in your life who will love you no matter what you do. I have heard some describe heaven as a place where you can do no wrong and where you are unconditionally loved, irrespective of what you do or say. Think of these people or that place when you feel tight and are unable to perform. You can envision your smiling spouse, mother, father, significant other, or child. I have even thought sometimes of Sugar, our incredibly calm and loving golden retriever. Allow that unconditional love to permeate through your body, and practice your ability to feel it first at rest while just sitting or lying in bed one night. Then practice it while performing or practicing your trade or sport without pressure. Once you start to become familiar with how to do it, try to employ it while performing under pressure. Allow their unconditional love for you to circulate through you, knowing that even if you lose—even if you choke it all away and perform terribly—they will still be there for you and love you unconditionally.

When I woke up in a cot by her side in the morning in the hospital, Lorraine didn't care how ragged I might have looked or whom I might have operated on the night before. She just wanted me there.

Check Your Ego at the Door

When I was five or six years old and had a baseball game, I would often get up incredibly early in the morning and throw on my uniform—sometimes ten hours before the game. I would run around the house, excited to play. I had almost no ego, just a pure innocent love of the game.

When I was twelve and played on the all-star team, I still dressed at home before my baseball games. But now, I spent a lot more time carefully adjusting my socks, sliding pants, and long-sleeve shirt. I got my "swag on," and with it I also applied several heavy layers of ego on top of my jersey. If my brother or sister messed up my hair or uniform, I responded like a spoiled egotistical major-league superstar, instead of what I was: a marginal Little League shortstop who was probably better fitted to playing second base.

As I grew older, I got dressed before my high school and college games at my locker in the locker rooms. But I still applied those same multiple heavy coats of ego as I dressed. It dripped from every orifice when that uniform was on, but I learned to apply it just a little bit closer and closer to the game time. Soon, I only applied it when I stepped in between the white lines of the field.

When I became a surgeon, I traded in the white chalk that outlined the baseball field for the red tape that marked the sterile environment of the operating room. I still get dressed in my uniform in a locker room surrounded by other combatants, only now the uniform I don is surgical scrubs instead of a baseball uniform. The playing field is an operating room, not a baseball or football field or a hockey rink. My batting helmet is replaced by a headlight. Yet the opponent, rather than being just another athlete on a rival team, is disease, cancer, and even death itself—which has no ego.

I still apply my ego as I suit up, but despite the increased seriousness of the challenges I now face, I've learned to apply fewer and fewer coats. Most importantly, I've learned to leave off the parts of the ego that are not necessary for me to do my job—or that prevent me from treating my teammates well.

A patient wants and deserves a confident surgeon, but arrogance and hubris are close neighbors. As an athlete, a performer, and eventually a super performer, you must learn that the inner confidence you must have in order to perform well under pressure can be applied later and later in the pre-event phase and immediately stripped and erased in the post-event phase. In fact, it can—and should—be applied in such a way that only you are aware of it even being on. In my opinion, this may be the most important concept and technique in this book: Your ego doesn't need to be applied so that everyone—or even anyone but yourself—is aware of it. Ego does not have to be applied in several thick coats, and it doesn't need to include any elements that lead you to show up your teammates when their performance is not up to your standards. Over time, by keeping your ego to yourself, it becomes easier and easier to enact a "we-centered" ego rather than a "me-centered" one.

Ego can be sometimes disguised under an air of modesty. A true "we-centered" super performer can still make big decisions in a moment: how to handle a multimillion-dollar deal, how to know where to throw or kick the ball at a crucial moment, how to make life-and-death decisions in the operating room. But you can still make these kinds of decisions with a confidence that exists only in between your ears and that does not need to be displayed in any way outside of that field, because the game is truly, ultimately played only in your mind. Your ego does not have to be noticeable to others in the arena.

You can tell whether or not you're checking your ego appropriately by paying attention to your own process of getting ready to perform. Once you've gotten ready—once you've put on your uniform and painted on your ego—ask yourself whether or not you treat others differently after that point. Once you are game ready, does your manner of interaction with other people—and especially other team members—change? For most of us, it does. It does for me.

Ask your team members these questions. An anonymous 360 evaluation from your colleagues is the one of the best ways to obtain true and honest information about yourself in these situations. Most of us do not really know the true answers to these questions until they're asked in a safely anonymous manner.

Once you have obtained honest and accurate information about how you treat those around you, start to consider how you can shrink your ego as you get closer and closer to the event. By this, I don't mean you have to change your pregame preparation; as I've stressed throughout this book, this remains crucial for success and should start days or even months before the event. However, your "performing ego" can be applied later and later and in fewer and fewer layers, until eventually it becomes invisible to those around you.

Over time, I've learned this technique: how to shrink the lines of the playing field to a smaller and smaller area, until eventually those lines exist only in my mind. You can learn this too—to check your ego not only at the door, but also between your ears.

Why Do We Fall?

In the movie *Batman Begins*, Alfred the butler—played so beautifully by Sir Michael Caine—asks: "Why do we fall, Master Bruce? So we can learn how to pick ourselves back up." Sometimes we learn best from our mistakes. Sometimes we learn best only after we fall down for one reason or another.

That's one movie quote, and here's another. In 1970, George C. Scott won an Oscar for playing the role of Patton.

In that movie he said, "Americans love a winner and will not tolerate a loser." For a long time, that quote meant a lot more to me than the Michael Caine quote ever could.

I've always had a problem with losing. As a boy, whenever I lost a competition or failed to meet a goal, I would replay the loss over and over in my mind. I relived every minute and asked myself what I could have done differently to have won. Embarrassingly, even as an "adult," after losing a second-grade Catholic sign-up basketball game coaching seven-year-old kids, I was no better.

Losing in the operating room to cancer is another loss that's hard to digest. I recall the first time I came out of an elective operation as an attending surgeon and had to tell the wife that the lung cancer we were treating had spread and there was a metastatic lesion on the diaphragm. This meant that the cancer was not curable, and that taking out the lung would be of no help. There was nothing we could do to win. So we just closed the patient's chest and I went out to talk to the family. The wife looked down and started to cry, and her daughter embraced her as I told them the bad news. I could offer nothing now beyond my prayers and support. I told them that I hoped the patient would respond to chemotherapy and radiation. Above all, I told them I was sorry that I had let them down.

Then, the daughter's adorable little six-year-old girl with ponytails, the patient's oldest grandchild, tugged at my surgical scrubs and said, "It's okay, doctor. You did not let us down—you did the best you could."

We had lost; her grandfather was going to die of cancer, and there was nothing I could do about it. Yet, incredibly, she, at six years of age, was consoling me.

The finality of that patient's experience still haunts me today—as does my experience on what was and still is the worst professional day of my life.

I was doing a high-risk robotic lobectomy in a patient who'd had previous chest irradiation. I got into bleeding from the pulmonary artery, which initially appeared to be easily repairable. But the patient bled more than usual, so we decided to open in order to fix the problem.

However, we discovered once we had opened that the patient had unknown hypertension on the right side of the heart, and as we were trying to fix that, the left side started to fail as well. We finished the operation, but he died later. Talking to his wife and beautiful family was horrible. I cannot even imagine their pain or loss.

Why Don't Professionals Have Coaches?

Again, it was a loss, and again, I brooded on it. I was not even sure if I could operate the next day. If it were my son or a player on a team that I coached, I could give him some words of experience. But like most surgeons, I had no coach.

It is interesting that most professionals don't have a coach. In fact, very few of us do outside of professional athletes. Why? Why don't lawyers or doctors or CEOs or business executives have coaches? Why don't accomplished leaders in their field have a coach? Yes, we as physicians have to go to courses and take refresher classes and read journals in our field, and every few years we must recertify ourselves before a board. But few of us have a coach to help us maximize the effectiveness of these usual practices. It makes little sense when you think about it, especially in light of the fact that we are operating on human beings and many professional athletes are just throwing or catching a ball or object.

Hiring a coach is not realistic for most of us, so we have to learn how to be our own coach. If you run a company or work with others, you may have to ask those around you to critically evaluate you in an anonymous way. You will never receive honest feedback from them if they think their comments may be identified. Thus you should use a 360 evaluation and ask those who work above you, below you, and alongside you to evaluate you. Think of it as an objective scale to evaluate your own performance.

Another method of being your own coach is to seek out other experts in your field and ask them how they perform their job and how they evaluate their performance. This strategy can sometimes work in unexpected ways. Recently, after I had separated my children from one of their typical silly arguments and knew I had to punish them, I asked them, "If you were the father here, if you were me, what punishment would you give your son?" Their answers gave me insight into how they think and how they want me to discipline them.

And something about the connection we formed after I'd asked them that question must have taken hold, because fortunately for me, the night after my patient had died and I wasn't sure I'd be able to operate the next day, my sixteen-year-old son Alec was able to step up and serve as my coach. He told me the same thing that I had told him for several years.

"Be a man, Dad," he said. "So you had a bad day; so what? You have been incredibly successful in the past. Be a man and go back on the field and perform and stop feeling sorry for yourself."

At first I was taken aback because my own words were coming back at me. Lorraine admonished Alec at first. But he was exactly right, in an insightful way. I have learned a lot more from losses than from wins.

It is often difficult for us to be self-critical. The advantage of having a coach is that he or she can view you in an objective manner and see you in a different way than you can see yourself. The advice becomes depersonalized. The advantage of videotaping ourselves, as described at length in a previous chapter, is to see ourselves as others see us. It is still amazing to me to see the reaction people have when they first watch themselves giving a lecture or operating. They can't believe how they look or sound. True, honest self-critical analysis is difficult, so call in your coach alter ego to help you.

After a loss or failure, act like a coach. Analyze your loss, and actually write down what you learned from that loss.

Ask yourself what you can do better next time to get a better outcome. Every failure is an opportunity to get better. Every failure is actually a blessing, and although it is always hard to see it this way at the time, the sooner you view the loss in this light the sooner you can turn the loss into a win.

When you get a poor result, do not accept that unconditional love and support from your family and friends who too often say that there was nothing else you could have done. Be like Alec was to me. Quite often when we discuss our failures or other bad outcomes in our lives with our family members, we and they conclude that there was nothing else we could have done differently. Often, this is because we have slightly tainted the story's facts to favor this conclusion. But the reality is that there is almost always something else you could have done differently. It may not have changed the results, but it's still important to be aware of, and it's still important to carefully consider the idea and all of the branch points of each decision. Do not make it too easy for yourself to start believing that the decision wasn't your fault. Accept accountability for the poor outcome, for your own actions and for the actions of your team, and work to improve the process.

A key component of this is the part about accepting accountability for the actions of your team. Currently my son Robby as a junior in college has an ERA (earned run average) in the Ivy League of 0.63, yet his win-loss record is 1–4. I've watched many of his games on the web and have even seen a few in person, and yes, there have been many errors behind him. But what I want him to learn is not to bemoan those errors, but how to make those men behind him play better when he is pitching.

I do this in my work as well. In the operating room, I noted that I was making a few of my nurses, who act as my bedside assistants, nervous when we were bringing the stapler and maneuvering it around blood vessels. This is the most anxiety-provoking part of the robotic lobectomy. Thus we had a practice session in which we developed a simple communication system. I could tell the bedside assistant how best to bring the stapler, and they could tell me what they were experiencing. This quickly elevated us as a team, and everyone got better quickly.

Find new and inventive ways to reach those around you in order to make them and your team better. A true MVP makes others around them better. This is not just a line from ESPN; it is true.

They Can't Stop the Clock

Although it is clear to me that one error cannot lead to another unless you let it, there are some days when a series of unrelated events out of your control just seem to go wrong. On any given day, you might just be unlucky. Usually, you don't discover this fact until you are long into your performance at work, at home, at school, or in the operating room. At this point, mental toughness is required to finish the day.

On one such day, I said to the resident: "Okay, we are

struggling in this operating room with a giant bloody tumor, we just got called for an emergency consult upstairs on a patient, there is a patient coming into the emergency room with a perforated esophagus in about one hour, and my wife just told me that her car needs major repairs. But there is good news—they can't stop the clock. At some point, this day is going to end."

The fact that time doesn't stop clearly isn't *always* good news, but on truly unlucky days, it's a comfort. We may not get much sleep tonight or even get to bed at all, but the smoke will clear, the sun will rise, we will eventually finish all the work, and the day will end. And tomorrow will—almost always—be better.

When days like this occur, it's important to have an optimistic attitude like this. Too many people are pessimistic; they almost expect bad luck, and when they get it, their attitude tells them that more is coming. "Oh, wouldn't you know it, just my luck!" That attitude is not for super performers. We have great luck and we expect great luck because we have worked hard to make our breaks go our way. And when things go against us, we know that our preparation means that "bad luck" will be brief and short lived.

As I've said many times before, you should critically assess seemingly "unlucky" events to ensure that they all were truly out of your control. Be overly critical and consider whether there was anything you could have done to prevent any of them. But once you are completely sure that they are out of your control, it's good to realize that we are all unlucky at some point. A true super performer continues to work hard, continues to prepare for every detail, and knows that soon his "luck" will change. It changes because you have continued to do the work that provides "good luck."

Yet sometimes, it is good to remind ourselves that this day or series of unlucky events will end. The movie *Cast Away* is one of my favorites because it displays the mental toughness of a man alone on an island for years. He says that he knew what he needed to do: "Just keep breathing; the sun will rise, and who knows what the tide will wash in." So focus on finishing the day with class and grace, knowing that the day will get better.

Knowing When to Stop

Lorraine left the hospital a few days after her mastectomy. She did great. We presented her cancer situation to oncologists at three major cancer centers and all of them agreed that she would be best served by several doses of three chemotherapies. This would increase her chance for cure from 85 percent to maybe 91 percent.

The night before she was to receive her first chemo, we were both scared of the unknown. We did not know what it would feel like for her to have chemotherapy drugs flowing through her veins. You would think that my experience treating cancer and her experience of administering chemotherapy to so many patients when she was a nurse at the Mayo Clinic would make us experienced. It did not. We prayed together that night. I knew the good Lord would take care of her. I kissed her and hugged her tight and said what I had said to her every night for over twenty-two years: "I love you, wifey, I will always love you, and I will always be here for you."

But I was afraid for the first time. Would she be okay? Would she be able to do all of the things she had been doing every day and that she loved to do: cooking, picking up the kids, volunteering at the schools? As I contemplated our future, I thought of ways in which I could be a better husband and father.

Finally, we fell asleep hugging and facing one another as we did during our first year of marriage.

Six weeks later, by the time her third dose of double chemotherapy was scheduled, she was a pro, a seasoned veteran of a club that not many want to be in. We had stopped talking about our fears, and now we only talked about our schedules, who was picking up the kids after their activities, and what was for dinner. Despite our travails, the world just kept spinning.

She never missed a day of doing her job. Even on the days she got chemotherapy, she shopped, did laundry, did the dishes, and even did some housework. She went to most of the kids' games, and she cooked enough the day before her chemotherapy sessions so that we would have leftovers. She even made a few trips "with the girls" in between treatments. I was learning from her courage, grace, and humility. All this time, I had thought that I was the super performer of the family, but it turns out to have been her the whole time. We as a family tried to see the silver lining in the whole experience of Lorraine's cancer. As I've described, I was a better doctor, and her experience made us both appreciate each other and each day together a bit more. It made our lives a bit kinder and the road we traveled together a bit easier. Somehow, the arguments at home over trivial matters were reduced, and they essentially disappeared.

However, experience can serve as a double-edged sword. It can both can enlighten and cloud an issue, even difficult intraoperative decisions like when a surgeon has to decide when to close a patient's chest and leave a cancer in or when to try to remove it.

When performing lung cancer surgery, if a second-level lymph node (called an N2 lymph node) has cancer in it, the benefit of removing the lung cancer is very controversial. Sometimes it is best to proceed with the operation and remove the lung and the cancer in it, but some patients are best served by our stopping the operation and leaving the lung cancer in and then treating the patient with radiation and chemotherapy. I am considered an expert on this intraoperative decision-making process and have written and lectured extensively about how to best manage N2 disease.

Yet sometimes, despite our great experience and expertise, we may still get it wrong from a family's perspective. Sara was a sixty-seven-year-old patient with lung cancer. I had her chest open and I had just heard from the patholo-gist that the second-level lymph node I sent in for frozen section analysis had cancer in it. Now it was decision time. We and Sarah's family had discussed this situation at length preoperatively, just in case. She had a handsome husband and twin blond granddaughters. I could stop and leave her cancer in and give her chemotherapy and radiation, or I could proceed and remove the lung cancer now and accept the risk of bleeding, shortness of breath, and many other complications with unproven benefit. Thus I elected to stop the operation.

Over the next few weeks Sarah had many complications from the chemotherapy, and she ultimately died. Her hus-band called me and was angry.

"Why did you stop, Dr. Cerfolio? Why did you leave my wife's lung cancer in and let her die? We came to you because you were supposed to be the best in the world—the Michael Jordan of lung cancer surgery—and yet you left her cancer in." He cried over the phone. She had just died last night. "I miss her so. Maybe if you had removed the cancer she would be here today, sitting by my side. The last two months were the worst times of our lives. The chemo made her so sick—that's what killed her. Not the cancer."

Was he right?

To ease his pain—and to explain to myself why I had decided to do what I had done—I told Sarah's husband a story about a patient named John.

Just four months earlier, I was faced with a similar decision when we also found a metastatic N2 lymph node while doing a procedure on John. John was much younger than Sarah, and he had a young family and one cute blond-headed daughter, no grandchildren. We also talked preoperatively to him and his family, and as with Sarah and her family, John wanted me to be aggressive. "That is why we flew to you from California, doctor, to have you as our surgeon," John had said. "We have heard that you are the best in the world, and very aggressive."

So that day, I didn't stop. John was young and had great pulmonary-function tests, and we knew he could tolerate the operation well. So I attempted to remove his very large and central cancer. But during the dissection, I got into bleeding from his pulmonary artery. The pressure in the right side of his heart was high. The only way to fix it and remove all of his cancer was to go on a bypass machine, so we did this. We sewed up the pulmonary artery, got the bleeding stopped, and got all his cancer out. But the right side of his heart failed, and John could not come off of bypass. Because of this, he died. I was devastated, and I had to go out and tell his wife and young family.

I still remember his daughter, who asked after I told them that her father had gone to another world, "What happened, Mommy? What is wrong? Is Daddy okay?"

And her mom had to tell her, "Daddy is never coming home again."

Imagine how they felt. They had come to us—to me— because we were supposed to be the best. I was supposed to get him through it, to deliver a perfect product. We prided ourselves on doing just this, or trying to. But in this case, we did not.

As soon as the operation on John had finished and I had told the family what happened, I returned to the operating room and called Lorraine. "I'm done," I said. "I'm done with this whole business of surgery. I'm getting out of it. I just can't do this anymore."

But before I could quit, I had two more operations to do that day and nine the next. One patient was already asleep under anesthesia waiting for me to start the operation. I had little choice but to go on. I had a job to do and patients relying on me, on us, to get it done. And eventually, of course, I didn't quit. Still, that moment in the operating room when I was ready to walk away from my entire career would be something I would not be able to let go of for a long time. It was an impetus for me to write this book.

In retrospect, should I have stopped with John and gone ahead with Sarah? Did I get them both wrong or both right? These are the questions that many surgeons face every day. We live with the consequences of these decisions every day. And, much more importantly, so do our patients and the families. We use literature and evidence-based medicine to help guide us, but each patient is different, and at the end of the day we rely on our experience to help us make the right decision.

Experience reduces our anxiety of the unknown. It helps us better understand what is coming and what to expect. If we have been in a situation before, we will know how to act because we have literally done it before. Further, we can draw on our experience from other situations in order to apply it to new ones.

However, sometimes no matter how much we know, no matter how many times we have been there before, there is no clear-cut right decision. In these situations, a super performer knows that the outcome may be unfavorable, but he or she must live with the results of his or her choice at the time. Hindsight is not always 20/20.

But we can always learn how to better apply the experience that we have acquired from other new situations. When a new and stressful situation is upcoming, we can write down all of the similarities that this new scenario has to ones we have experienced in the past. By writing it down, we can create a clear argument that the new scenario isn't totally new after all; there are many aspects of it that we may have dealt with before. A lecture to ten people is not that different from one to a thousand people. It is the same voice and same message, just a different audience. It's the same with an athletic performance. A playoff game has the same rules to it as a regular-season game. The pregame pomp and circumstance do not make the game itself different, only the atmosphere, and the number of seats around the field doesn't change the dimensions of the field itself. A lobectomy on a poor farmer is the same as a lobectomy on a famous politician or actor. And in particular, a decision made on behalf of Sarah was largely the same as a decision made on behalf of John.

Given my experience, I would make the same decisions again for both Sarah and John, even though in practice neither outcome was favorable. But Lorraine's experience taught us both how to live with our decisions and their consequences, whether these were right or wrong.

Lorraine was a super performer, and our lives went on. She did well with her chemotherapy, and eventually she made it through. Her beautiful blond hair slowly grew back, she had reconstructive surgery on both breasts, and she physically healed. Our family slowly healed emotionally as well. We even went on another Royal Caribbean family cruise, and Lorraine and the boys outperformed me on a tree-climbing exercise, the Treetop Adventure in Saint-Martin. It seemed, at last, that our lives were back to normal.

It was on that cruise that I wrote the initial outline for this book, as well as its first sentence. In my mind, the book was complete. It was to be about how surgery was like life and sports, and how experience can help us get better and better in all aspects of life. It was to be about how we learn to perform under pressure, how we as individuals go through a process of personal growth from childhood innocence; to adolescent insecurity, hubris, and arrogance; and finally to becoming a team player and a finely tuned athlete who can super perform in all aspects of life. And it was to be about how challenges at work and in life help us to grow individually and allow us to bring home lessons to teach our children so that they can travel a less-circuitous pathway to super performing than we, ourselves, had to.

As you'll see—and maybe have seen—it ended up being about more than that. There was more of the story yet to come.

Losing Is an Opportunity to Get Stronger

It was the first travel AAU basketball team that I ever coached, and we were playing the final game in a tournament. Alec was only eleven. We were ahead with three minutes to go, but turnovers killed us, and we lost.

When the game ended, I looked at the young boys sitting on our bench. Some were crying, and some were just hanging their heads. Rather than give them the usual colloquial lines—"You have nothing to hang your head about," "We had a great season and lots to be proud of," etc.—I asked them to sit quietly on the bench and watch the other team celebrate. I asked them to think about what we could have done better in practice—not in this game, but in practice—to have changed the outcome. I asked them to watch and ingrain the images of the other team's celebration in their minds so they could remember how this loss felt.

"Taste the loss," I told them. "Roll it around in your mouth for a while. Swallow it slowly. Watch them celebrate. Watch them hoist your trophy over their heads while you hang yours."

I was doing just the same. Maybe if I had changed my defensive scheme, it could have been different. Maybe I should have slowed down the game even more or made one or two different substitutions. I brooded on those last three minutes in my mind for months and just could not forgive myself for not coaching better and giving my players the chance to celebrate.

After my patient John died, I returned to my office for a brief minute before I had to go back to operating. I had just called Lorraine, telling her that I wanted to quit, and she was supportive and sweet to me as always. But as I described, I needed to get mentally ready for the next patient, who was already in the operating room, being prepped and draped.

I was sitting in my chair and had my headlight still on my head, which was hanging in shame just as my players' heads had been. I was shocked at what had just happened. How could that happen to me—the bleeding, the right-heart failure, having to go onto bypass, the talk with the loving and caring family who just lost their husband, their father, their brother? But it was over. I could not change it; it had happened. We did not know that he had right-sided heart failure or high pressure in the pulmonary artery. All of our preoperative tests were normal. It wasn't anyone's fault, and I needed to forgive myself and move on—but how could I do that? John's family couldn't go on; they would never be the same. I could still see his wife's face, the big tears rolling down that cute little girl's cheeks because her father had just died.

I thought about this as I sat in my office. And as I looked up I saw a picture, a picture that had been in my office for over ten years. Lorraine gave it to me a long time ago, and I had placed it on my shelf and forgotten about it. It was dirty and dusty and had been pushed off into the corner, barely visible from the window shade. But it was still there; I had never removed it. It was not the first time I had looked at it, of course, but it was the first time I had looked at it after feeling the way I did. The photograph depicts Jesus standing behind a surgeon. The heavenly figure's hand is gently and unassumingly positioned on the surgeon's right hand and helping to guide it.

This image helped me go back to the operating room and perform the way I knew I could, the way I knew I had to, the way my patient and every patient deserved their surgeon to perform.

The event shook me to my core and even made me question all that I knew, or thought I knew. For the next several days, I was not as confident. That week Rob Headrick, an outstanding cardiothoracic surgeon and good friend of mine, came to the OR to watch some surgery. He could tell I was off my game a bit, and we talked for a while about what we do every day as surgeons. Rob said, "If we do not do it, who will?"

He was right: Who else had the training and toughness to get back on the horse after having a bad outcome? It's true that on some level, we had been uniquely chosen and trained for this job, but we're still just humans, and the toll is high. It's important to emphasize that: We are all human, and we all lose. Losing comes in many different forms. As young children, we have to learn that losing is part of life and that losing is a learning opportunity. Those two facts are often hard to learn. You need to start to spin a loss immediately as an opportunity to get better, or maybe to prepare differently the next time. You have to view it as a chance to grow and to capitalize on the experience of the loss. As soon as you have learned that you did not get accepted or you were not chosen, you need to seek information as to why. Use that information to try to identify your areas of weakness. If there was a judge or a board that made the decision, be proactive and ask them why you were not selected. Too many people think that information of this kind is not available, but if you seek it out aggressively, it may be. Armed with that information, you can critically review your performance and improve yourself. A loss is a great opportunity, but only if you see it in that light and then do the work to capitalize on it.

Too often I hear coaches say what I said years ago: Roll the taste of that loss around in your mouth and remember what it is like. This is right, but it's only half of the equation. In order to execute this strategy, you have to have tried your hardest, prepared your best, and still lost. And then you have to be smart enough to recognize the opportunity you were given by losing.

You also have to be smart enough to forgive yourself more readily. This may seem like the polar opposite of the main theme of this book, which has largely recommended tough self-criticism, honest self-inspection, and the desire to get better. Most super performers possess many of these qualities and already do this to some extent. However, few of us forgive ourselves well enough or quickly enough when we make a mistake. This is especially true of surgeons.

It is also important to be humble enough to let others help you at these times as well. This is important not only because other people can help you better than you can help yourself; as a super performer, you are also allowing other people to help you, and this process makes them feel better about the loss as well. If you are truly interested in helping others, your acceptance of their help will help both you and them.

Being able to be humble in this way comes down to knowing the difference between when to be self-critical and when you need to forgive yourself. Although the latter is rare, there are times when you have to be able to see the line between the two. If you truly prepared absolutely as well as you could have, and if you truly performed the best you could, and if you still lost, then you need to forgive yourself for the loss. Walking around and feeling sorry for yourself does not allow for healing or improvement. In fact, it prevents it. No one is going to be 100 percent perfect. Therefore, when you're going into any high-pressure performance, you need to know that you may make a mistake or two. In fact, you should expect them to occur and prepare your mind in advance to forgive yourself for them and to move on so that you can continue to perform.

And you have to know that sometimes you are going to lose no matter what you do. You have to accept this, forgive yourself for the loss, and move on. Obviously, this is easier to do if you've lost a baseball game than if you've failed at a business decision, which may cost your company millions of dollars, or if you've failed in an operation, which means that a patient has died. But whatever the stakes, we need to understand before going into the game that a loss is always possible.

When you are a busy surgeon and you have seven or eight operations a day, or when you're a Major League Baseball player with a 162 games a year, or a corporate executive who has five meetings a day, it is difficult to see each challenge as a unique opportunity. As super performers, we all understand that it is hard to do what we do every day, week after month after year. However, as we discussed earlier, if you see today as the last day of your life—if you realize the frailty and finality of events—you might have a different perspective. How would you view your job if you knew that tomorrow something would happen to take it away from you forever? By embracing that perspective, each day or event takes on a new life of its own. Your day will go by quicker and you will feel more enriched.

To feel pressure in a situation only means that the situation is important to you. Realize how lucky you are to have the chance to perform under pressure each day. Enjoy it, embrace it, and look forward to it. We are lucky that we get to do something every day that creates the concept of pressure and has a level of expected, professional performance. One day as a surgeon I will have to retire and hang up the scalpel, and this day usually occurs sooner for surgeons than for a medical doctor because of the physicality of our job. One day, my job won't be there for me, just as one day it won't be there for you.

To help stay in this perspective, you can write down how you want to be remembered on the day of your funeral, and then you can write the eulogy someone might deliver you if you were to die today. If your eulogy doesn't match how you'd like to be remembered, then you have work to do. The good news is that you have time. Right now, today, you can start acting in a way that will decide how others will remember you, no matter how you may have acted in the past. All of us have a finite number of days left in our lives to compete against others, to work with others, to help others, to struggle for a cause worth fighting for, and even to get paid for doing it. Because of that finality, make each day and each human-to-human interaction count.

This—as it turned out in the end—is one of the major lessons my wife taught me.

CHAPTER 8

Super Performing Is
Just a Piece of the Puzzle

Super Performing to Serve Others

. . .

Losing with Grace

The Reason to Want
to Be a Super Performer

Lorraine and I sat on the plane with our three boys seated in
the row behind us. It was March of 2012, two full years after
her breast cancer surgery and after her chemotherapy was
over. Lorraine was cancer free, and we were happy as a family.

Our hard work, it seemed, was paying off. I was now doing
more robotic chest surgery than anyone else in the world, and
we were consistently coming up with new ways to perform
it better, as well as new ways to teach it. Robby was premed

at Yale and was doing well in school and in baseball as their number-one pitcher; Alec was named the captain of the high school baseball team and had a GPA of 3.9; and Matthew had made the varsity baseball team as a freshman in high school and had a 4.1 GPA his first semester. Most importantly, Lorraine's most recent CT scans showed no evidence of cancer. It seemed as if her cancer was behind her now, and life was moving on. As individuals and as a family, we were super performing and happy.

We were traveling on this plane because I was going to teach my advanced robotic surgery course to four surgeons and their teams from around the world in Celebration, Florida, near Orlando, as I did every few months. Neither Lorraine nor the boys had ever come with me before while I was teaching this course. We had always been too busy before. But now, Lorraine thought—and I agreed—that we might take a few days to celebrate life, but for me it was to celebrate Lorraine's health and our good fortune.

Lorraine decided to combine my lecture with a three-day vacation for all of us to Disney World and MGM Studios. She knew I hated vacations that were longer than four days, but if you combined it with my work, then I would go for it. And I did. Lorraine loved Disney World. The kids thought she loved it for the same reason they did—for the rides—but in truth, she loved it because it got us together. It gave us time to check all of our busy lives for a few days and just be a family, as we seemed to have more time to do when the boys were young and life was simpler. Now we were all so busy with school, our exercise and lifting routines, and sporting events that it was hard to find time for even a truncated family vacation.

We had a great time. I seemed to enjoy this vacation better than any other, despite the fact that it was one of our least expensive. Lorraine's scare with cancer made me appreciate our time together now more than ever. Her illness had matured me in several ways. Her cancer made me understand the fragility of life better, the finiteness of my life with my family, and the pleasure each day could provide. I appreciated my roles better as a husband, a father, and even a doctor, and so I prepared to enjoy each day of the rest of my life more than ever.

This is where this book was supposed to end. This was to be my last chapter when I wrote the outline: "And we all lived happily ever after, and I learned so much about life." But life went on.

Understand Your Higher Purpose

Later that year, in November, Lorraine called me from an airport. She had been with Matthew all weekend for a baseball tournament when she developed severe back pain again. She couldn't even walk.

A month earlier, she had experienced this pain, but her CT scan showed everything as being normal. When we reviewed the first scan later, we realized that there was a large, bony lesion visible on the scan, but it had somehow been missed.

Now, in November, Lorraine had a bone scan, PET scan, and second CT scan. This time, the results were not good. She had four lesions in her bones: one in her back where her pain was, one in her rib, one in her pelvic bone, and one in her right arm.

The next step was to get a tissue biopsy, but there was a conflict. We had a trip coming up to the Southern Thoracic Surgical Association. I had been named president a year before and I was to be inducted, with Lorraine honored as the first lady. Her role was to help set up some of the logistics of the meeting for the next year and help select the band, the food, etc. She was looking forward to it and happy to forget about her problems for a few days and get the rest of the biopsies and work up later. Still, we wanted to get a tissue biopsy and diagnosis done before the trip, but a needle biopsy was inconclusive, and we assumed it was metastatic breast cancer. So we decided to go on the trip we had planned for months and do the biopsy a few days later when we got back home.

So we went. We told only a few close friends about her bony lesions and the pain she was having. She never complained about pain, cried, or felt sorry for herself during this entire trip, and she managed her pain with only Motrin. At the ceremony, she smiled and looked stunning in her ballroom gown. We had a great time and even took a walk on the beach one afternoon and listened to music on our iPhones. We played the song "100 Years."

When we got back home, the biopsy results did not show the metastatic breast cancer as we had been expecting. Rather, it was something much worse. The tests were positive for the bony form of leukemia, called a chloroma. This meant that Lorraine had acute myeloid leukemia, or AML—and it was a bad form of AML. Her AML had actually been caused by the chemotherapy that the doctors had given her back in 2010 for the breast cancer. The chance of getting this cancer from chemotherapy that is supposed to treat cancer is about 1 in 500. This made her prognosis even worse: She now had only a 20 to 30 percent survival rate.

Lorraine was in tears and devastated as the doctor told us the news in the clinic. She asked the doctor: "I want to dance at my children's weddings, I want to watch my boys graduate from college, I want to live. Can I?"

Our perfect world had changed again. Once again, cancer had invaded our Camelot. And this time, the chemotherapy she was to receive would be more toxic than ever. Lorraine knew what was coming. She said two years earlier that she never would go through chemotherapy again and lose her hair, but she knew it was her only chance to stay alive for her boys. So before her first chemotherapy, she shopped for Christmas gifts for the boys and for me.

She did her job, even when she was critically ill and fighting for her life. She understood her greater purpose in life.

She was super performing even when facing her own mortality. She had given up her career to serve her family; she had even given up her identity to be a mom. She was always serving others, especially her family members.

It was Christmas Eve. Lorraine had been in the hospital since December 12, getting huge doses of severely toxic chemotherapy. We tried to keep our lives as normal as possible. The boys were taking their tests, playing their sports. I was still working, operating during the days and spending each night in the hospital sleeping by my wife's side. I sat by her side along with many of her friends, and I slept in the hospital every night, as did her closest friends, Jan, Nanette, and Sheri. I had not been home in a few weeks. Alec and Matthew—then sixteen and fourteen—were essentially on their own at home during this time. I canceled most of my lectures and trips except for the ones that involved teaching other surgeons. Robby had come home from college for Christmas break.

That Christmas Eve, Lorraine and I sat in her hospital bed together and called home on our iPad to FaceTime our boys. She had prepared for her illness and for her chemotherapy. Her preparation for her family always astonished me. We watched them open up the gifts at home from her hospital bed—gifts that she had bought them before going into the hospital. It made her happy to see the boys enjoy them.

It reminded me of the last time I saw a well-wrapped gift opened in the hospital: It was 1995, the day our second son, Alec James, was born. Just after his birth, Lorraine had me go to her bag and grab something. I was confused: What could be in her bag, and who cared about some gift? In her bag was a gift that she had brought. The gift actually was for Robby, who at that time was about two and a half. She gave it to Robby and said, "Robby, this gift is from your new brother. His name is Alec. He loves you." I was amazed by her then and now. I had not even thought of doing such a thing.

This Christmas Eve, though, we were less joyous. Lorraine was in tears once the call ended. She said her job as a mom was to be home on Christmas Eve and that she had failed her children. But there was no way she could have been home. Her white-blood-cell count was still almost zero and she had a fever. She was too weak. So we spent Christmas and New Year's Eve together in the hospital. But I did not care because I was with her. I understood my role as a surgeon and as a husband as well.

Her role became even clearer to me in February 2013. She had been home for only two weeks in all of 2013 to that point. Her cancer was not responding well to the chemo, and each bone marrow biopsy she had yielded results that were worse than the one before, despite the increasing toxicity of the chemo that she was receiving daily. A bone marrow transplant was her only chance for a cure, but the stakes were high.

We got a ray, a beacon of hope: She had two perfect transplant matches in her brother Michael and her sister Karen. But her bad test results delayed her transplant date further and further.

She finally got out of the hospital in mid-February and had a few good weeks at home. She was doing okay; she was shopping and cooking and doing all the things she loved to do. Most of all she was happy because she could be a mom again and a wife again. She loved those roles. Her beautiful blond hair was, of course, all gone from the chemotherapy, but she was happy to be home.

During this respite, she even felt well enough to travel. Her white-blood-cell count was up, and her fever was down. So we decided to travel to Florida to watch Robby pitch a spring-training game for Yale. Yale was playing Army, and Robby was to be the starting pitcher. The game would be played at the New York Yankees' training facility in Tampa, Florida, and several scouts were coming to watch Robby pitch.

We flew there the night before the game and had dinner with our son and my mom and dad. Robby was thrilled to see his mom and to see how well she looked. She did not divulge her pain or other problems. The next day, we got to the ball-park early and walked around the stadium and the Yankees' complex. Lorraine was weak. It was hot, and she complained only to me about her wig and her back pain. But she thought only of Robby.

"I wonder if he is hungry," she said. "I wonder if he has sunblock on his neck."

She was a mom first and a patient second. She cherished that role.

She decided to try to see Robby before the game, but I told her Coach Stuper did not want the kids talking to their parents before the game. Still, she walked down behind the grandstands to the space behind the dugout. She saw Robby coming out of the bathroom. She gave him a turkey sandwich, and she applied sunblock to his neck so that his hands would not get greasy.

Robby pitched well. He threw 6 and ⅔ innings and gave up only one earned run, and all of that on only two legitimate hits. Robby was pulled from the game in the seventh inning. He walked off the field with class, despite the score at the time showing him down 2–1. Several scouts were there, and one came up to me and said, "I have seen a lot of gutsy performances, but even with all those errors behind him, your son showed great class and never got onto his teammates."

The most important event, though, was Robby seeing his mom before we had to head back to the airport. The taxicab was waiting at the baseball park. I watched Lorraine get Robby's attention on the top of the dugout and wave good-bye to him. He smiled and waved back. I wish now that he could have run out of the dugout and hugged her and given her a kiss good-bye, but that would have been unprofessional. That entire day, despite her physical pain, Lorraine understood her role as part of the team, as the matriarch of our family. She was there for her son. She understood her greater purpose.

Our roles in life change and evolve. Eventually, we learn that our higher purpose is often to be the most valuable member not *of* the team, but *for* the team. Individual performances are meaningless unless we have someone to share them with.

It's important to see your role in your job, your organization, your team, or your family as just part of a bigger picture. See how you can expand it to better your organization. My wife did this better than anyone I have ever meet. She did it while she worked as a nurse, and she did it in her role as a mother. It wasn't a job she was getting paid to do, but it was the one she valued the most by far.

To do the same, you have to think outside of yourself. You need to look hard sometimes to see it, but your performance in many roles affects the lives of many others. Your attitude affects their performance as well. Even if you are a solo golfer in a tournament or the sole proprietor of a business, your performance and the decisions you make from day to day affect the lives of others.

Make sure you fully evaluate the effects of your decision in one role on the other roles we all hold. For example, if you decide to stay late to work and miss coming home for dinner, your role as a father and spouse suffers. Prior to making a decision, carefully consider the consequences that decision will have on the other roles you serve. Then ask yourself what is the most important role you serve. Ensure that that role is preserved first and be faithful to it first.

We all employ metrics of how well we are doing at work. These metrics carefully and accurately measure our job performance with objective data. Surgeons, for example, track thirty- and ninety-day mortality rates, length of hospital stays, blood loss rates, etc. All of those, as I stressed earlier in this book, are objective, measurable metrics. But do you have these objective metrics for your role as a husband or wife or as a father or mother? Write down the number of Little League games you miss each year or the number of times you missed the kids' school play. Record the times you take your partner out for dinner or for a movie, just the two of you. Then see if you can improve on your score each year by using objective, measurable data for the most important roles in your life.

The Power of Prayer

Despite our island of calm in mid-February 2013, Lorraine's prognosis continued to get worse each week. As soon as we returned from our trip to see Robby, Lorraine was readmitted to the hospital. She was dehydrated and sick, and the doctor told her that her chance for a cure had now fallen to 5 to 10 percent at best. He said the next line of chemo would be even worse: It would be even harder on her and make her even sicker. And, he cautioned us, it probably would not work. The other option was to go home and die at peace with her family by her side.

Lorraine said, "Doctor, I want to dance at my children's

weddings; I want to watch them graduate from college; I want to watch them grow old. I'll try the new chemo."

After the doctor left, we hugged one another and cried together and prayed. But she kept fighting.

During these horrible months I kept operating, teaching, and lecturing. I had to support her and be there for her but I still had a job to do. Still, I cancelled my visiting professorships to Brazil and Spain. Lorraine was supposed to go on both of those trips with me, and we had been so excited to get some time alone together. But she could not go now.

I never missed a day of work. I operated every day and removed cancer from my patients. Often I would think of Lorraine as I scrubbed just before surgery. I thought of her incredible class, courage, and dignity through this entire ordeal. She never complained to the nurse or doctors. They all just loved her, just as everyone else in her life did. The problems we had in the OR that always seemed so insurmountable and made me so frustrated in the past were now so miniscule compared to what my wife was going through just four floors above me.

Thus her spirit and resiliency strengthened me as well. I was a bit kinder and gentler, and I better understood what the patients—and especially what their families—were going through. I had a better understanding of what it meant to sleep in the hospital as a family member, to eat all of your meals in the hospital, to shower and shave there. I better understood what it was like to walk around each day and think about your spouse's life and what life would be like without them.

One day I was doing a lobectomy, and the resident was struggling to dissect out the pulmonary vein from the tissue around the heart. Instead of getting angry with him or lambasting him for struggling over what seemed so simple, I thought of Lorraine's kind smile despite her illness and her incredible kindness to her nurses. And so I was more patient and understanding. I took him slowly through the steps of how to do it. I was kinder and gentler to him and to other members of my team.

Lorraine's illness changed me in other ways as well. In the South, many families like to pray with the patient just before they go to the operating room. In the past, I would often ask my nurse to hurry this process along so that we did not hold up the surgery. Now I was more likely to go into the holding area and pray with the family and patient just before the patient was wheeled into the operating room.

The art and concept of praying to a higher being has been around for a long time—as far as we know, for as long as human beings have been on the planet.

Prayer doesn't require a church or even a religion. Even if you are agnostic, the mere act of praying helps ease your mind and spirit and comforts and relaxes you. Yoga is a form of praying, in a way. Whatever method you choose, the idea that you are not alone and that things outside your control happen for a reason provides comfort even in the most difficult situations. The vast majority of athletes across the world seem to share this belief.

For me and Lorraine, our faith and prayers are the central pieces, the cornerstone and hallmark of our lives and of our performances. The good Lord is with you—you are never alone.

Grace, Dignity, Humility, and Faithfulness

Lorraine never yelled at the doctor and never complained or questioned his treatment. She was never angry with God. One day, a resident came in and was visibly upset with the news that despite all the therapy Lorraine was getting, she was doing so poorly. Lorraine—the patient in her hospital bed, incredibly ill and sick—actually consoled him.

"It's okay, doctor," she told him. "You have done your best. Don't be disappointed—we will get it with this next round of chemo, and we'll do the bone marrow in April. I will do a better job for you."

But her AML continued to spread, and with a vengeance. Her fever climbed, and her white-blood-cell count remained zero.

The world kept spinning, and the boys and I, as super performers, all had commitments to honor. We honored them. I still operated every day and ran upstairs to have dinner with her every night and sleep by her side.

After dinner, sometimes, we walked around the hospital. I showed her where I went in between operations. I showed her the call room that I was showering in, and she even made rounds with me a few times to see some of my patients. The patients loved seeing my wife standing in the hallway dragging her own IV pole. They all asked: "What's wrong with her, doctor? She looks so beautiful; she can't be too sick. Is she going home soon?"

Lorraine never told the kids about her terrible pains or about the full severity of her problems. She did not want to distract them from their schoolwork, baseball games, or other duties, she said. She just smiled in that quiet Mona Lisa way that only she could smile, and she said nothing. We would FaceTime the kids most nights, but some nights, if she did not think she looked good, we would only call. We made sure that they were doing their homework. Her friends were so sweet and brought over meals many nights for the kids and even to us in the hospital. Her closest friends were there by her side every day, day after day, week after month.

The entire month of March, Lorraine was in the hospital getting toxic high-dose chemotherapy. The bone marrow was put on hold again and again—this time, until April 22—because she always needed more chemo. More chemo, more tests, and every day more bad news. Lorraine—my wife, my life—was losing her battle, our battle, with cancer, but she kept fighting. I now knew that she might not survive, but she did not want to talk about it with me. She was not ready to give up.

Each day, Lorraine woke up hopeful and smiling, and each day and night she prayed and prayed on her rosary. I often would lie in bed at night and ask God how this could have happened, how could it have happened to Lorraine? But Lorraine's faith was unrelenting, unwavering.

One night, we were watching the miniseries *The Bible* on TV in her hospital room, when the scene of Doubting Thomas came on. I looked over and saw she was crying. I climbed into her bed and hugged her. "Why are you crying?" I asked.

"I never want to be like Thomas," she said, "never. And I thought I never would, but I have prayed and prayed so hard to get better every day for my family, and none of my prayers have been answered. Every test has been bad, every prayer has been unfulfilled." And then she paused and said, "But I know God will answer my prayers one way or another. I know he is with me, even though I cannot see him or put my hand in his. I know he will answer my prayers in his own way, even though I do not see him."

That is how I felt that day in the operating room, and this is how I felt this day with my wife. Early in my life, I just could not accept the no-win scenario. I could not. I had to always try to think of a novel way to win—I had to win. But this time—in the most important battle of my life, the battle to cure my wife's cancer—I was losing. No matter what we did, no matter what I did, no matter what doctor's opinion I sought from all over the world, no matter whom I spoke to on the phone or by Internet, we were losing.

Lorraine and I wanted to handle these events with grace and kindness to the doctors and nurses. She did.

When we talked to the kids, they would tell her to keep fighting and that they were proud of her. The word *quit* did not exist in our house, but maybe it should have. Sometimes it is good to know that you are going to lose and then learn to lose with class. Sometimes, when another team beats you, you have to know the game is over and tip your cap to them, smile, shake their hands, and congratulate them.

Then—you can always tell yourself in a game—you'll wait until next year to win. But when the opponent is cancer, there is no next year.

Sometimes, no matter what you do, you will lose. We all lose in life. Even when you lose, you can be kind and understanding. If it is a sporting event, this is easy. Even in a business deal, if you have lost millions of dollars, you can lose with class—and if you do, it may help you later with the next deal. They may be impressed with how you lost and be more likely to consider you for the next time.

When a loss is inevitable—and first you must ensure that the loss is 100 percent inevitable—then you should learn to accept the loss even during the end of the competition or process. I have seen this change in the National Basketball Association in the past five years. Now, when players on either the winning or losing team know the win or loss is inevitable, they often will dribble out the clock for the last thirty seconds to one minute. They all recognize that the game is over and want to acknowledge the other team's victory with class.

Just as you prepare your response to winning, you should prepare in advance your response to losing. This process needs to be mentally installed in you before the event. One key method after you realize that the loss is inevitable is to think of all the people who lost with you. Think of each team member and what the loss will mean to them. As Lorraine's disease progressed, I thought of her nurses, who loved her and who took such great care of her every day, minute after minute. I thought of them and how they were feeling. Thank everyone who's losing with you the second you lose. Thank them for their efforts, consider their feelings, and console them if you can.

All of this is much harder to do, of course, when you're losing a battle with cancer—when you're losing your life. But Lorraine showed me that even then, you can lose like a super performer—which means to lose with class.

Life and Death

It was Wednesday, April 10, 2013. I thought back to the first time I ever saw Lorraine: It was also a Wednesday, in September of 1988, at the Saint Francis Hospital cafeteria in Hartford, Connecticut. I remembered how I could not stop looking at her across the cafeteria; how, when I spoke to her, I couldn't keep from staring deep into her beautiful blue eyes and smiling. They were so blue, so beautiful. All I wanted to do now was look into her eyes for hours, but I could not. I had nine operations this day, and Lorraine was still in the hospital, where she had been for over two months now.

I was still doing my job best I could as a dad, as a husband, and as a surgeon. I was on top of my game in the operating room, despite everything. But it felt different, after Lorraine's illness, to be on top of my game.

There is no level of achievement that prevents failure or a loss. Despite all the operations I had done, all the bleeding I had been in, and all the tough spots I had sewn my way out of, I could still lose it all. I could lose my skill in an instant; my experience guaranteed me nothing the next day. Similarly, all the praying that Lorraine had done, all the exercises we did as a family every day, the fact that she never smoked, she never drank, she was never overweight, and she worked out almost every single day I knew her—none of this protected her from getting breast cancer and then getting AML from her chemotherapy.

You can prepare perfectly for a game and still lose. No one's family is immune from cancer; no degree of faith or amount of prayers, no money, no educational status could totally prevent it. We had climbed a mountain together through Lorraine's illness—we understood, together, that other side of super performance at last. I was operating better than ever, in a way, because I now had the vantage point from the top of that mountain, the perspective both of the patient and of the doctor. And I now wanted more than ever—sad, in a way, as it may sound—for other surgeons to get to this point.

After I finished my operations and rounds that day, Lorraine and I had dinner together. We talked and laughed. We watched *Jeopardy!*, and even then she could still beat me.

The next day was Thursday, April 11. The time had come for me to travel back to Florida for about eighteen hours to teach my advanced robotic course. By now I was teaching other full-fledged attending surgeons—and even professors at major medical teaching centers—how to perform our methods of surgery, not just residents or fellows, and I had to keep that commitment. But with my wife sick in a hospital bed, I needed to make this teaching trip short, and I needed to maximize my time with her before my flight at seven thirty p.m. We talked for a long time, and I remembered the first long conversation I'd had with her back in September 1988 at the hospital in Hartford. That day, when I had to leave to catch my flight, I wanted to do nothing more than go back to her hospital bed and talk to her about those same things all over again. But I couldn't.

In Florida, I checked into the same hotel we had stayed at as a family just barely a year ago to celebrate what we had thought of as the defeat of Lorraine's cancer: the Melia Hotel in Celebration. I called Lorraine: I wanted to see how her vision was, since she had bled behind her retina a day ago. But the first thing she asked me was what room I was staying in. I told her it was the same room we had as a family, the room they always gave me when I was here teaching. The suite seemed so empty without her. She cried and wished she were with me there, as healthy and happy as she had been just a few months ago. She did not want to FaceTime because she had a patch over her eye from the bleed and she believed she did not look good. I had asked two retina specialists to see her. They said there was nothing they could do. She might never get that vision back, they told me. It was more bad news and another loss, another possible long-term disability from the cancer.

I taught my course and flew back to Birmingham. I got back to Lorraine's room on Friday, April 12, 2013, by five p.m. "I am so glad you are back," she said when I came into the room. "I knew it would be the typical R. J. Cerfolio sub-twenty-four-hour trip." And she smiled in that way that only she could, that quiet, unassuming, but captivating Mona Lisa smile.

I had asked Lorraine's mom, dad, sister, and brother and his family from Connecticut to come to Birmingham for the weekend to see her and to spend time with her. When I was arranging this visit the week before, Lorraine wondered why I was bringing them in. She asked whether it was because I thought she was going to die soon.

"No, honey, not at all," I told her. "I just want them to see you and spend some time with you. You have not seen them in almost a year."

She still did not want to discuss her possible death. Those conversations seemed to give her anxiety, despite her strong belief, and she did not want to openly discuss the concept, so we never did.

Her mother was ninety-three years old and her dad was eighty-nine, and both of them had health issues. But they came along with her sister Karen, her brother Chris and his wife, Robin, and their son Charles. They arrived Friday night. They spent an hour with her, but both she and they were tired. Lorraine had a continuous pain pump infusing morphine into her body now, and she was in less pain, despite increasing complications due to her illness. Matthew was supposed to come and visit her as well, as he usually did on Friday nights, but she told him not to come because she didn't want him to see her in pain. She didn't want her children to know how bad some of her symptoms actually were, so we never told them.

I spent that Friday night with Lorraine. We both loved Friday nights. Our first date was on a Friday night, back in September 1988. I took her to dinner in Hartford, Connecticut. It was the first time we ever kissed, and I still remember the magic I felt.

Lorraine got a good night's sleep. Lorraine's friend Sheri slept in her room, and I slept in the call room down the hall. I woke early the next day. It was Saturday, April 13, 2013. We had gotten married on a Saturday: November 10, 1990. I rounded quickly on my patients and ran up to have breakfast with her. She looked good, she felt better, and the pain was less.

While we ate, Lorraine told me to listen to what Sheri had seen last night. Sheri told us how she had awoken in the middle of the night with a feeling that a nurse was in the room checking on Lorraine. She peered up and saw a large male figure leaning over Lorraine. It was no nurse, but the shadow of what looked like an angel, its wings partially opened. Lorraine was asleep, but she stirred with Sheri moving, and as Lorraine turned, the angel vanished.

"It was beautiful," Sheri said. "It was her guardian angel, and it came here to help protect her."

Sheri knew that I was a scientist, but she also knew that I had a deep faith as well. The story and concept gave us both warmth and comfort. It made Lorraine feel safe. Lorraine smiled as Sheri told me the story, as did I. I knew I would never see an angel. Angels do not appear to someone like me, but I was glad one was with my wife, watching over her.

I had my online MBA class from eight to eleven a.m. I had listened to it online at Lorraine's bedside every Saturday morning for that whole year while Lorraine slept, and today was no different. When it finished, I told her that we needed to walk to help get her ready for the bone marrow. "You are doing great now," I said, "and I want you to be in the best shape you can." After one lap, I asked her if she was up for one more. I pushed her to make two full laps around the entire ninth floor because I knew she had to get ready in order for the transplant to be successful. She was exhausted, but she did not complain. While we walked, I thought about how tomorrow was Sunday: The first day we had ever walked on the beach together was a Sunday, just as we had done after the Southern Thoracic Surgical Association dinner in November. It seemed so long ago.

When we finished walking, Lorraine was tired. Her platelets were low, and I was afraid she might bleed into her retina again, so I pushed for the doctors to quickly infuse her platelets, and they did. The bone marrow was planned for the next week, and we were hopeful that after that, at last, she might be on the road to recovery.

When we finished walking, it was time to watch Robby's game over the Internet. That day, Robby was the starting pitcher against Harvard at a game in Boston. My mom and dad, as well as my two sisters, Laverne and Nina, and my youngest sister Laverne's husband, Tim, had all traveled there to watch Robby pitch. Robby and I had prepared on the phone the night before and gone over how to pitch to each batter in their lineup. Lorraine spoke to him the morning of the game as well. She told him to pitch well, to have fun, and that she loved him. She never told him about her pain, loss of vision, or recent problems. She did not want him to lose focus or worry about her before the game.

I was excited and ready to score the game and record every pitch, as I always do. But Lorraine told me that she was tired, and that she wanted to sleep.

"But we always watch the games together, honey," I said.

"No, honey, not now, not today," she replied. "I am so exhausted, and I just want to sleep."

I began to protest, but she continued. "I have taken you away from Alec and Matthew; they have been all alone for so long. I have taken you away from your workouts in the sun that I know you love. I have taken you away from the lawn. Go home to the boys, please, go home to our boys and do what you love, work out in the sun, and cut the grass. My parents are coming in at two. I'll sleep until then."

After I put up a little resistance, I left; she needed to sleep. I leaned down and kissed her and said what I had always said every night for twenty-two years: "I love you, wifey. I will always love you, and I will always be here for you."

She said, "I know, and I love you too."

I wish I knew then that this was to be the last time I would see her alive or get to talk to her or see her beautiful blue eyes. But I did not. I left. I left her alone. I abandoned her in that hospital room all by herself.

Her family came in from two to five p.m., and they said she slept almost the entire time. She was peaceful, they said, and not in pain.

I was home cutting the grass, making my lines of gratification in the lawn just as I had done when I was a boy. I was proud of them, and I was making them so that when I drove Lorraine home from the hospital after her transplant in just a few days, she could see them and be proud of me. Just then, my pager went off. Jessica, Lorraine's nurse, told me something bad had just happened to Lorraine. She said Lorraine had hit the call button, screamed, and then could not talk. I grabbed Matthew and we rushed into the hospital.

By the time I got there, Lorraine had been transferred to the intensive care unit (ICU). I saw the CT scan of her brain. Almost the entire frontal and parietal lobes of her brain were full of blood. It was not a survivable injury. We rushed into the ICU, and there was my beautiful wife, my love, my life on a ventilator with blood pouring out of her nose. She was essentially brain dead, with only the ventilator keeping her alive.

How do you tell your sons that their mother is brain dead and going to die within a day? You just tell them. I called Robby in Boston, and he started telling me about how well he had pitched—but this day, his performance was not quite so relevant. I had him and my family members, who were with him in Boston, fly to Birmingham immediately. Alec, the captain of the high school baseball team, actually missed a baseball game to go to Florida to compete in a national honor choir. He told me how they took third in the country, but I interrupted him with the shocking news. Robby and my family arrived late that Saturday night at eleven p.m., and Alec flew in the next morning at eight a.m.

That Sunday morning, we were all there at her bedside, most all of her family and friends. We all sat by her bedside and held her hand and prayed as we turned the ventilator to a lower setting.

Lorraine loved the TV show *Lost*. We all did. When you asked her why she loved *Lost* so much, she said, "Because it brought my family together so well. We all watched each new episode each week, and we talked about it and discussed our theories. It was one hour when my whole family got together, had fun, and shared an interest, a culture. We discussed the meaning of life almost every week." I used my phone to play the theme from *Lost* called "Life and Death" as her heart rate and respiration rate fell. I whispered in her ear as her spirit left the bonds of this world into the next: "I love you, wifey. I will always love you, and I will always be here for you." And then I whispered something else for her, and for her alone to hear.

As "Life and Death" played, Lorraine's body passed away, but her soul soared to start her new life. It was 10:23 a.m., April 14, 2013.

My life, my wife was gone from this world. It was a Sunday. The first time we ever prayed together was a on a Sunday. How I wished I could hold her hand and pray together again with her now, but I could not.

The wake was Tuesday, and on Wednesday morning, a few hours before her funeral, I decided that I needed to give her eulogy. I did not think I could do it; I was not sure I could perform under the insurmountable grief. But this book is about just that—about super performing under pressure—and she deserved it and more. So I did. Although I had given hundreds of lectures all over the world, this was by far the hardest one

I ever gave. But I did it for her. She deserved so much better than me, but now she was experiencing what her whole life had been about: her afterlife. I was not sure what I was going to say or how I was going to keep myself composed. It took all of the strategies in this book plus more. My children have since added slides to my eulogy and placed it on YouTube.

In my eulogy, I spoke about what Lorraine taught us—and still does, most every day. I spoke about her faithfulness, her humility, and her perseverance in a cause that is based on love and goodness toward others. This was the platform of her life. Her life was predicated on her love for her children and for me. For all of us who knew her, her actions made the trail to a meaningful and more loving life easier to follow every day. Even today, when the kids are arguing or fighting, I ask them, "Is that what your mother would want you to do or say right now?" This makes them stop and think about their mother and what her life represented. They act less selfishly when they think of her because of the way she lived her life.

The funeral was on Wednesday, April 17. It was just after Saint Bernadette's day. Lorraine's mother did not give her a middle name at birth, so Lorraine got to choose one for herself as her confirmation name. She chose Bernadette. She loved to watch or read any story about Saint Bernadette of Lourdes. Lorraine suffered great pain, like Bernadette, and like Bernadette her faith never wavered. It rained the day Lorraine was born, it rained the day we got married, and despite it being a beautiful sunny day when her funeral started, it rained as the pallbearers and my boys and I carried her casket from the white hearse to her gravesite. It was Lorraine's rain.

The major lesson I want to impart to you in this book, now that a large part of my story, in some ways, has ended, is this: Realize that your time on this planet is finite. The path and message you leave and the number of people you positively influence is totally up to you. We all stumble and fall during our journey; we all make mistakes and take wrong turns—me more than most. So keep blazing your path toward your goal, but do not forget to help those behind you find their way. Each time you reach a destination, look over your shoulder to see who is struggling behind you, and help them along to join you on the summit. That, in the end, is what Lorraine helped to teach me.

EPILOGUE

The Mastery of Pursuits
That Offer Endless Significance

On Friday, April 19, 2013, two days after Lorraine's funeral and my eulogy, I had four visiting surgeons from Asia who had already flown in to Birmingham, Alabama, to watch my team and me perform robotic surgery. My kids had school and tests and baseball games that weekend. Robby had to fly back to Yale and pitch against Dartmouth on Saturday. Alec and Matthew went back to school and had baseball games to compete in as well. I had to go back to work. Life went on—the world kept spinning—but to me, it seemed to spin a bit slower. We all had commitments to fulfill.

As I operated that Friday, I spoke to Lorraine in my mind the entire time. I had never thought of someone as much as I have Lorraine that day, or for many days since. When she was here, I just assumed that she would always be here for me, that we would grow old together. But I was wrong. Now, every few seconds, her beautiful face and voice popped into my mind. I narrated the entire operation to her and performed it in her honor. I used the incredible love I had for her to make me stronger and to help me perform better—to super perform.

I knew in my heart that she was and still is here with me by my side, that somehow she can see me. I hope I make her proud. I know that she is guiding my hand and giving me emotional and physical strength to take care of my patients, to be gentler and kinder, and to be a better father to our boys. In short, to be more like Lorraine.

As I write this, it's been three months since Lorraine died, and I think about her as often now as I did on that Friday. Throughout the process of writing, the direction and meaning of this book has changed to some extent, but Lorraine's death drives home the most salient point of all: High performance without a noble cause or purpose is worthless. It is not just the endless pursuit of mastery that matters, but rather mastery of pursuits that offer endless significance. It has to be based on a noble cause that is driven by love and goodness, and it has to be shared with others. My nobler cause has been to continue to operate and help patients, to teach others how to operate, and to be a better father, doctor, friend, and man.

The purpose of this book is for you to find your higher calling and your nobler cause. It may be sitting right in front of you now, or it may require a journey in order to discover.

Either way, your path to super performing is not complete without an honorable cause for which you will perform.

I will miss Lorraine and will always love her. But my knowledge that she is at peace soothes me. It helps me perform in the operating room and at home. There is no word, no emotion, and no way to convey the depth of my loss. It is infinite, and the emptiness inside of me is permanent. But each month, it becomes a bit easier to bear. I will never be the same, but I will heal, and I will be even better. Life goes on, and Lorraine would want me to raise the boys as she did: with love, helping them find happiness in their lives and a higher calling. And I will—I will do it for Lorraine Bernadette Mojcik Cerfolio.

ABOUT THE AUTHOR

Robert J. Cerfolio, MD, MBA, is currently the James H. Estes Family Endowed Chair of Lung Cancer Research and Full Professor Chief of Thoracic Surgery at the University of Alabama in Birmingham. He received his medical degree from the University of Rochester School of Medicine, his surgical training at the Mayo Clinic and at Cornell-Sloan Kettering hospital, and has been in surgical practice for more than twenty-six years. "Cerf," who was a First Team Academic All-American baseball player in college, is now a world-renowned chest surgeon and well recognized as one of the busiest and best thoracic surgeons in the world. He has performed more than 15,700 operations, written 160-plus original papers and 60 book chapters, and delivered better than 300 visiting professor lectures worldwide. Hundreds of surgeons and their teams have come from all over the world to watch Cerf and his team perform complex thoracic and robotic operations and to learn how he motivates his teammates to model and deliver excellence day after day.

Made in the USA
Middletown, DE
09 August 2020